AF619590

The Old and New Testaments: A Progressive Revelation of Christ in Scripture

John Calvin; Caleb Sinclair

GRAPEVINE INDIA

Published by

GRAPEVINE INDIA PUBLISHERS PVT LTD

www.grapevineindia.com
Delhi | Mumbai
email: grapevineindiapublishers@gmail.com

Ordering Information:
Quantity sales: Special discounts are available on quantity purchases by corporations, associations, and others.
For details, reach out to the publisher.

First published by Grapevine India 2023

CONTENTS

1. THE LAW GIVEN, NOT TO CONFINE THE ANCIENT PEOPLE TO ITSELF, BUT TO ENCOURAGE THEIR HOPE OF SALVATION IN CHRIST, TILL THE TIME OF HIS COMING.

From the deduction we have made, it may easily be inferred, that the law was superadded about four hundred years after the death of Abraham, not to draw away the attention of the chosen people from Christ, but rather to keep their minds waiting for his advent, to inflame their desires and confirm their expectations, that they might not be discouraged by so long a delay. By the word law, I intend, not only the decalogue, which prescribes the rule of a pious and righteous life, but the form of religion delivered from God by the hands of Moses. For Moses was not made a legislator to abolish the blessing promised to the seed of Abraham; on the contrary, we see him on every occasion reminding the Jews of that gracious covenant made with their fathers, to which they were heirs; as though the object of his mission had been to renew it. It was very clearly manifested in the ceremonies. For what could be more vain or frivolous than for men to offer the fetid stench arising from the fat of cattle, in order to reconcile themselves to God? or to resort to any aspersion of water or of blood, to cleanse themselves from pollution? In short, the whole legal worship, if it be considered in itself, and contain no shadows and figures of correspondent truths, will appear perfectly ridiculous. Wherefore it is not without reason, that both in the speech of Stephen and in the Epistle to the Hebrews, that passage is so carefully stated, in which God commands Moses to make all things pertaining to the tabernacle "according to the pattern showed to him in the mount." For unless there had been some spiritual design, to which they were directed, the Jews would have laboured to no purpose in these observances, as the Gentiles did in their mummeries. Profane men, who have never seriously devoted themselves to the pursuit of piety, have not patience to hear of such various rites: they not only wonder why God should weary his ancient people with such a mass of ceremonies, but they even despise and deride them as puerile and ludicrous. This arises from inattention to the end of the legal figures, from which if those figures be separated, they must be condemned as vain and useless. But the "pattern," which is mentioned, shows that God commanded the sacrifices, not with a design to occupy his worshippers in terrestrial exercises, but rather that he might elevate their minds to sublimer objects. This may be likewise evinced by his nature; for as he is a Spirit, he is pleased with none but spiritual worship. Testimonies of this truth may be found in the numerous passages of the Prophets, in which they reprove the stupidity of the Jews for supposing that sacrifices possess any real value in the sight of God. Do they mean to derogate from the law? Not at all; but being true interpreters of it, they designed by this method to direct the eyes of the people to that point from which the multitude were wandering. Now, from the grace offered to the Jews, it is inferred as a certain truth, that the law was not irrespective of Christ; for Moses mentioned to them this end of their adoption, that they might "be unto God a kingdom of priests;" which could not be attained without a greater and more excellent reconciliation than could arise from the blood of beasts. For what is more improbable than that the sons of Adam, who by hereditary contagion are all born the slaves of sin, should be exalted to regal dignity, and thus become partakers of the glory of God, unless such an eminent blessing proceeded from some other source than themselves? How also could the right of the priesthood remain among them, the pollution of whose crimes rendered them abominable to God, unless they had been consecrated in a holy head? Wherefore Peter makes a beautiful application of this observation of Moses, suggesting that the plenitude of that grace, of which the Jews enjoyed a taste under the law, is exhibited in Christ. "Ye are," says he, "a chosen generation, a royal priesthood." This application of the words tends to show, that they, to whom Christ has appeared under the gospel, have obtained more than their forefathers; because they are all invested with sacerdotal and regal honours, that in a dependence on their Mediator they may venture to come boldly into the presence of God.

II. And here it must be remarked, by the way, that the kingdom, which at length was erected in the family of David, is a part of the law, and comprised under the ministry of Moses; whence it follows, that both in the posterity of David, and in the whole Levitical tribe, as in a twofold mirror, Christ was exhibited to the view of his ancient people. For, as I have just observed, it was otherwise impossible that in the Divine view they should be kings and priests, who were the slaves of sin and death, and polluted by their own corruptions. Hence appears the truth of the assertion of Paul, that the Jews were subject, as it were, to the authority of a schoolmaster, till the advent of that seed, for whose sake the promise was given. For Christ being not yet familiarly discovered, they were like children, whose imbecility could not yet bear the full knowledge of heavenly things. But how they were led to Christ by the ceremonies, has been already stated, and may be better learned from the testimonies of the Prophets. For although they were obliged every day to approach God with new sacrifices, in order to appease him, yet Isaiah promises them the expiation of all their transgressions by a single sacrifice, which is confirmed by Daniel. The priests chosen from the tribe of Levi, used to enter into the sanctuary; but concerning that one priest it was once said, that he was divinely chosen with an oath, to be "a priest for ever after the order of Melchisedec." There was, then, an unction of visible oil; but Daniel, from his vision, foretells an unction of a different kind. But not to insist on many proofs, the author of the Epistle to the Hebrews, from the fourth chapter to the eleventh, demonstrates in a manner sufficiently copious and clear, that, irrespective of Christ, all the ceremonies of the law are worthless and vain. And in regard to the decalogue, we should attend to the declaration of Paul, that "Christ is the end of the law for righteousness to every one that believeth;" and also that Christ is "the Spirit," who gives "life" to the otherwise dead letter. For in the former passage he signifies that righteousness is taught in vain by the precepts, till Christ bestows it both by a gratuitous imputation, and by the Spirit of regeneration. Wherefore he justly denominates Christ the completion or end of the law; for we should derive no benefit from a knowledge of what God requires of us, unless we were succoured by Christ when labouring and oppressed under its yoke and intolerable burden. In another place, he states that "the law was added because of transgressions;" that is, to humble men, by convicting them of being the causes of their own condemnation. Now, this being the true and only preparation for seeking Christ, the various declarations which he makes are in perfect unison with each other. But as he was then engaged in a controversy with erroneous teachers, who pretended that we merit righteousness by the works of the law,—in order to refute their error, he was sometimes obliged to use the term law in a more restricted sense, as merely preceptive, although it was otherwise connected with the covenant of gratuitous adoption.

III. But it is worthy of a little inquiry, how we are rendered more inexcusable by the instructions of the moral law, in order that a sense of our guilt may excite us to supplicate for pardon. If it be true that the law displays a perfection of righteousness, it also follows that the complete observation of it, is in the sight of God a perfect righteousness, in which a man would be esteemed and reputed righteous at the tribunal of heaven. Wherefore Moses, when he had promulgated the law, hesitated not to "call heaven and earth to record" that he had proposed to the Israelites life and death, good and evil. Nor can we deny that the reward of eternal life awaits a righteous obedience to the law, according to the Divine promise. But, on the other hand, it is proper to examine whether we perform that obedience, the merit of which can warrant our confident expectation of that reward. For how unimportant is it, to discover that the reward of eternal life depends on the observance of the law, unless we also ascertain whether it be possible for us to arrive at eternal life in that way! But in this point the weakness of the law is manifest. For as none of us are found to observe the law, we are excluded from the promises of life, and fall entirely under the curse. I am now showing, not only what does happen, but what necessarily must happen. For the doctrine of the law being far above human ability, man may view the promises, indeed, from a distance, but cannot gather any fruit from them. It only remains for him, from their goodness to form a truer estimate of his own misery, while he reflects that all hope of salvation is cut off, and that he is in imminent danger of death. On the other hand, we are urged with terrible sanctions, which bind, not a few of us, but every individual of mankind; they urge, I say, and pursue us with inexorable rigour, so that in the law we see nothing but present death.

IV. Therefore, if we direct our views exclusively to the law, the effects upon our minds will only be despondency, confusion, and despair, since it condemns and curses us all, and keeps us far from that blessedness which it proposes to them who observe it. Does the Lord, then, you will say, in this case do nothing but mock us? For how little does it differ from mockery, to exhibit a hope of felicity, to invite and exhort to it, to declare that it is ready for our reception, whilst the way to it is closed and inaccessible! I reply, although the promises of the law, being conditional, depend on a perfect obedience to the law, which can nowhere be found, yet they have not been given in vain. For when we have learned that they will be vain and inefficacious to us, unless God embrace us with his gratuitous goodness, without any regard to our works, and unless we have also embraced by faith that goodness, as exhibited to us in the gospel,—then these promises are not without their use, even with the condition annexed to them. For then he gratuitously confers every thing upon us, so that he adds this also to the number of his favours, that not rejecting our imperfect obedience, but pardoning its deficiencies, he gives us to enjoy the benefit of the legal promises, just as if we had fulfilled the condition ourselves. But as we shall more fully discuss this question when we treat of the justification of faith, we shall pursue it no further at present.

V. Our assertion, respecting the impossibility of observing the law, must be briefly explained and proved; for it is generally esteemed a very absurd sentiment, so that Jerome has not scrupled to denounce it as accursed. What was the opinion of Jerome, I regard not; let us inquire what is truth. I shall not here enter into a long discussion of the various species of possibility; I call that impossible which has never happened yet, and which is prevented by the ordination and decree of God from ever happening in future. If we inquire from the remotest period of antiquity, I assert that there never has existed a saint, who, surrounded with a body of death, could attain to such a degree of love, as to love God with all his heart, with all his soul, and with all his mind; and, moreover, that there never has been one, who was not the subject of some inordinate desire. Who can deny this? I know, indeed, what sort of saints the folly of superstition imagines to itself, such as almost excel even the angels of heaven in purity; but such an imagination is repugnant both to Scripture and to the dictates of experience. I assert also that no man, who shall exist in future, will reach the standard of true perfection, unless released from the burden of the body. This is established by clear testimonies of Scripture: Solomon says, "There is not a just man upon earth, that doeth good and sinneth not." David; "In thy sight shall no man living be justified." Job in many passages affirms the same thing; but Paul most plainly of all, that "the flesh lusteth against the Spirit, and the Spirit against the flesh." Nor does he prove, that "as many as are of the works of the law are under the curse," by any other reason but because "it is written, Cursed is every one that continueth not in all things which are written in the book of the law to do them;" evidently suggesting, and even taking it for granted, that no one can continue in them. Now, whatever is predicted in the Scriptures, must be considered as perpetual, and even as necessary. With a similar fallacy Augustine used to be teased by the Pelagians, who maintained that it is an injury to God, to say that he commands more than the faithful through his grace are able to perform. To avoid their cavil, he admitted that the Lord might, if he chose, exalt a mortal man to the purity of angels; but that he neither had ever done it, nor would ever do it, because he had declared otherwise in the Scriptures. This I do not deny; but I add that it is absurd to dispute concerning the power of God, in opposition to his veracity; and that, therefore, it affords no room for cavilling, when any one maintains that to be impossible, which the Scriptures declare will never happen. But if the dispute be about the term, the Lord, in reply to an inquiry of his disciples, "Who, then, can be saved?" says, "With men this is impossible; but with God all things are possible." Augustine contends, with a very powerful argument, that in this flesh we never render to God the legitimate love which we owe to him. "Love," says he, "is an effect of knowledge, so that no man can perfectly love God, who has not first a complete knowledge of his goodness. During our pilgrimage in this world, we see through an obscure medium; the consequence of this, then, is, that our love is imperfect." It ought, therefore, to be admitted without controversy, that it is impossible in this carnal state to fulfil the law, if we consider the impotence of our nature, as will elsewhere be proved also from Paul.

VI. But for the better elucidation of the subject, let us state, in a compendious order, the office and use of what is called the moral law. It is contained, as far as I understand it, in these three points. The first is, that while it discovers the righteousness of God, that is, the only righteousness which is acceptable to God, it warns every one of his own unrighteousness, places it beyond all doubt, convicts, and condemns him. For it is necessary that man, blinded and inebriated with self-love, should thus be driven into a knowledge of himself, and a confession of his own imbecility and impurity. Since, unless his vanity be evidently reproved, he is inflated with a foolish confidence in his strength, and can never be brought to perceive its feebleness as long as he measures it by the rule of his own fancy. But as soon as he begins to compare it to the difficulty of the law, he finds his insolence and pride immediately abate. For how great soever his preconceived opinion of it, he perceives it immediately pant under so heavy a load, and then totter, and at length fall. Thus, being instructed under the tuition of the law, he lays aside that arrogance with which he was previously blinded. He must also be cured of the other disease, of pride, with which, we have observed, he is afflicted. As long as he is permitted to stand in his own judgment, he substitutes hypocrisy instead of righteousness; contented with which, he rises up with I know not what pretended righteousnesses, in opposition to the grace of God. But when he is constrained to examine his life according to the rules of the law, he no longer presumes on his counterfeit righteousness, but perceives that he is at an infinite distance from holiness; and also that he abounds with innumerable vices, from which he before supposed himself to be pure. For the evils of concupiscence are concealed in such deep and intricate recesses, as easily to elude the view of man. And it is not without cause that the Apostle says, "I had not known lust, except the law had said, Thou shalt not covet;" because, unless it be stripped of its disguises, and brought to light by the law, it destroys the miserable man in so secret a manner, that he does not perceive its fatal dart.

VII. Thus the law is like a mirror, in which we behold, first, our impotence; secondly, our iniquity, which proceeds from it; and lastly, the consequence of both, our obnoxiousness to the curse; just as a mirror represents to us the spots on our face. For when a man is destitute of power to practise righteousness, he must necessarily fall into the habits of sin. And sin is immediately followed by the curse. Therefore the greater the transgression of which the law convicts us, the more severe is the judgment with which it condemns us. This appears from the observation of the Apostle, that "by the law is the knowledge of sin." For he there speaks only of the first office of the law, which is experienced in sinners not yet regenerated. The same sentiment is conveyed in the following passages: that "the law entered, that the offence might abound;" and that it is therefore "the ministration of death, which worketh wrath and slayeth." For iniquity undoubtedly increases more and more, in proportion to the clearness of that sense of sin which strikes the conscience; because to transgression of the law, there is then added contumacy against the lawgiver. It remains, therefore, that the law arm the Divine wrath against the sinner; for of itself it can only accuse, condemn, and destroy. And, as Augustine says, if we have not the Spirit of grace, the law serves only to convict and slay us. But this assertion neither reflects dishonour on the law, nor at all derogates from its excellence. Certainly, if our will were wholly conformed to the law, and disposed to obey it, the mere knowledge of it would evidently be sufficient to salvation. But since our carnal and corrupt nature is in a state of hostility against the spirituality of the Divine law, and not amended by its discipline, it follows that the law, which was given for salvation, if it could have found adequate attention, becomes an occasion of sin and death. For since we are all convicted of having transgressed it, the more clearly it displays the righteousness of God, so, on the contrary, the more it detects our iniquity, and the more certainly it confirms the reward of life and salvation reserved for the righteous, so much the more certain it makes the perdition of the wicked. These expressions, therefore, are so far from being dishonourable to the law, that they serve more illustriously to recommend the Divine goodness. For hence it really appears, that our iniquity and depravity prevent us from enjoying that blessed life which is revealed to all men in the law. Hence the grace of God, which succours us without the assistance of the law, is rendered sweeter; and his mercy, which confers it on us, more amiable; from which we learn that he is never wearied with repeating his blessings and loading us with new favours.

VIII. But though the iniquity and condemnation of us all are confirmed by the testimony of the law, this is not done (at least if we properly profit by it) in order to make us sink into despair, and fall over the precipice of despondency. It is true that the wicked are thus confounded by it, but this is occasioned by the obstinacy of their hearts. With the children of God, its instructions must terminate in a different manner. The Apostle indeed declares that we are all condemned by the sentence of the law, "that every mouth may be stopped, and all the world may become guilty before God." Yet the same Apostle elsewhere informs us, that "God hath concluded them all in unbelief," not that he might destroy or suffer all to perish, but "that he might have mercy upon all;" that is, that leaving their foolish opinion of their own strength, they may know that they stand and are supported only by the power of God; that being naked and destitute, they may resort for assistance to his mercy, recline themselves wholly upon it, hide themselves entirely in it, and embrace it alone for righteousness and merits, since it is offered in Christ to all who with true faith implore it and expect it. For in the precepts of the law, God appears only, on the one hand, as the rewarder of perfect righteousness, of which we are all destitute; and on the other, as the severe judge of transgressions. But in Christ, his face shines with a plenitude of grace and lenity, even towards miserable and unworthy sinners.

IX. Of making use of the law to implore the assistance of God, Augustine frequently treats; as when he writes to Hilary: "The law gives commands, in order that, endeavouring to perform them, and being wearied through our infirmity under the law, we may learn to pray for the assistance of grace." Also to Asellius: "The utility of the law is to convince man of his own infirmity, and to compel him to pray for the gracious remedy provided in Christ." Also to Innocentius Romanus: "The law commands: grace furnishes strength for the performance." Again, to Valentine: "God commands what we cannot perform, that we may know for what blessings we ought to supplicate him." Again: "The law was given to convict you; that being convicted you might fear, that fearing you might pray for pardon, and not presume on your own strength." Again: "The end for which the law was given, was to diminish that which was great, to demonstrate that you have of yourself no ability to work righteousness, that thus, being poor, indigent, and destitute, you might have recourse to grace for relief." Afterwards he addresses himself to God: "Thus do, O Lord! thus do, O merciful Lord! command that which cannot be performed: even command that which cannot be performed without thy grace: that when men cannot perform it in their own strength, every mouth may be stopped, and no man appear great in his own estimation. Let all men be mean, and let all the world be proved guilty before God." But I am not wise in collecting so many testimonies, when this holy man has written a treatise expressly on this subject, which he has entitled De Spiritu et Litera, On the Spirit and Letter. The second use of the law he does not so clearly describe, either because he knew that it depends on the first, or because he did not so fully understand it, or because he wanted words to explain it with distinctness and perspicuity adequate to his ideas of it. Yet this first office of the law is not confined to the pious, but extends also to the reprobate. For though they do not, with the children of God, advance so far as, after the mortification of the flesh, to be renewed, and to flourish again in the inner man, but, confounded with the first horrors of conscience, remain in despair, yet they contribute to manifest the equity of the Divine judgment, by their consciences being agitated with such violent emotions. For they are always desirous of cavilling against the judgment of God; but now, while it is not yet manifested, they are, nevertheless, so confounded with the testimony of the law and of their own conscience, that they betray in themselves what they have deserved.

X. The second office of the law is, to cause those who, unless constrained, feel no concern for justice and rectitude, when they hear its terrible sanctions, to be at least restrained by a fear of its penalties. And they are restrained, not because it internally influences or affects their minds, but because, being chained, as it were, they refrain from external acts, and repress their depravity within them, which otherwise they would have wantonly discharged. This makes them neither better nor more righteous in the Divine view. For although, being prevented either by fear or by shame, they dare not execute what their minds have contrived, nor openly discover the fury of their passions, yet their hearts are not disposed to fear and obey God; and the more they restrain themselves, the more violently they are inflamed within; they ferment, they boil, ready to break out into any external acts, if they were not prevented by this dread of the law. And not only so, they also inveterately hate the law itself, and execrate God the lawgiver, so that, if they could, they would wish to annihilate him whom they cannot bear, either in commanding that which is right, or in punishing the despisers of his majesty. In some, indeed, this state of mind is more evident, in others more concealed; but it is really the case of all who are yet unregenerate, that they are induced to attend to the law, not by a voluntary submission, but with reluctance and resistance, only by the violence of fear. But yet this constrained and extorted righteousness is necessary to the community, whose public tranquillity is provided for by God in this instance, while he prevents all things being involved in confusion, which would certainly be the case, if all men were permitted to pursue their own inclinations. Moreover, it is useful even to the children of God, to be exercised by its discipline before their vocation, while they are destitute of the Spirit of sanctification, and are absorbed in carnal folly. For when the dread of Divine vengeance restrains them even from external licentiousness, although, their minds being not yet subdued, they make but a slow progress at present, yet they are in some measure accustomed to bear the yoke of righteousness; so that when they are called, they may not be entirely unaccustomed to its discipline, as a thing altogether unknown. To this office of the law the Apostle appears particularly to have referred, when he says, "that the law is not made for a righteous man, but for the lawless and disobedient; for the ungodly and for sinners; for unholy and profane; for murderers of fathers and murderers of mothers; for manslayers, for whoremongers, for them that defile themselves with mankind, for men-stealers, for liars, for perjured persons, and if there be any other thing that is contrary to sound doctrine." For he here signifies that it restrains the violence of the carnal desires, which would otherwise indulge themselves in the most unbounded licentiousness.

XI. But we may apply to both what he elsewhere asserts, that to the Jews "the law was a schoolmaster to bring them to Christ;" for there are two kinds of persons who are led to Christ by its discipline. Some, whom we mentioned in the first place, from too much confidence either in their own strength or in their own righteousness, are unfit to receive the grace of Christ, till they have first been stripped of every thing. The law, therefore, reduces them to humility by a knowledge of their own misery, that thus they may be prepared to pray for that of which they before supposed themselves not destitute. Others need a bridle to restrain them, lest they abandon themselves to carnal licentiousness, to such a degree as wholly to depart from all practice of righteousness. For where the Spirit does not yet reign, there is sometimes such a violent ebullition of the passions, as to occasion great danger of the soul that is under their influence being swallowed up in forgetfulness and contempt of God; which would certainly be the case, if the Lord did not provide this remedy against it. Those, therefore, whom he has destined to the inheritance of his kingdom, if he do not immediately regenerate them, he keeps under fear by the works of the law till the time of his visitation; not that chaste and pure fear which ought to be felt by his children, but a fear which is, nevertheless, useful to train them, according to their capacity, to true piety. Of this we have so many proofs, that there is no need to adduce any example. For all who have lived for a considerable time in ignorance of God will confess it to have been their experience, that they were constrained by the law to a certain kind of fear and reverence of God, till, being regenerated by his Spirit, they began to love him from their hearts.

XII. The third use of the law, which is the principal one, and which is more nearly connected with the proper end of it, relates to the faithful, in whose hearts the Spirit of God already lives and reigns. For although the law is inscribed and engraven on their hearts by the finger of God,—that is, although they are so excited and animated by the direction of the Spirit, that they desire to obey God,—yet they derive a twofold advantage from the law. For they find it an excellent instrument to give them, from day to day, a better and more certain understanding of the Divine will to which they aspire, and to confirm them in the knowledge of it. As, though a servant be already influenced by the strongest desire of gaining the approbation of his master, yet it is necessary for him carefully to inquire and observe the orders of his master, in order to conform to them. Nor let any one of us exempt himself from this necessity; for no man has already acquired so much wisdom, that he could not by the daily instruction of the law make new advances into a purer knowledge of the Divine will. In the next place, as we need not only instruction, but also exhortation, the servant of God will derive this further advantage from the law; by frequent meditation on it he will be excited to obedience, he will be confirmed in it, and restrained from the slippery path of transgression. For in this manner should the saints stimulate themselves, because, with whatever alacrity they labour for the righteousness of God according to the Spirit, yet they are always burdened with the indolence of the flesh, which prevents their proceeding with due promptitude. To this flesh the law serves as a whip, urging it, like a dull and tardy animal, forwards to its work; and even to the spiritual man, who is not yet delivered from the burden of the flesh, it will be a perpetual spur, that will not permit him to loiter. To this use of the law David referred, when he celebrated it in such remarkable encomiums as these: "The law of the Lord is perfect, converting the soul: the statutes of the Lord are right, rejoicing the heart: the commandment of the Lord is pure, enlightening the eyes," &c. Again: "Thy word is a lamp unto my feet, and a light unto my path;" and many others, which he introduces in every part of this psalm. Nor are these assertions repugnant to those of Paul, in which he shows, not what service the law renders to the regenerate, but what it can bestow upon man merely of itself; whereas the Psalmist in these passages celebrates the great advantage derived, through the Divine teaching, from the reading of the law, by those whom God inspires with an inward promptitude to obedience. And he adverts not only to the precepts, but to the promise of grace annexed to their performance, which alone causes that which is bitter to become sweet. For what would be less amiable than the law, if by demands and threats it only distressed the mind with fear, and harassed it with terror? But David particularly shows, that in the law he discovered the Mediator, without whom there is nothing pleasant or delightful.

XIII. Some unskilful men, being unable to discern this distinction, rashly explode Moses altogether, and discard the two tables of the law; because they consider it improper for Christians to adhere to a doctrine which contains the administration of death. Far from us be this profane opinion; for Moses has abundantly taught us, that the law, which in sinners can only produce death, ought to have a better and more excellent use in the saints. For just before his death he thus addressed the people: "Set your hearts unto all the words which I testify among you this day, which ye shall command your children to observe, to do all the words of this law. For it is not a vain thing for you; because it is your life." But if no one can deny that the law exhibits a perfect model of righteousness, either we ought to have no rule for an upright and just life, or it is criminal for us to deviate from it. For there are not many rules of life, but one, which is perpetually and immutably the same. Wherefore, when David represents the life of a righteous man as spent in continual meditations on the law, we must not refer it to one period of time only, because it is very suitable for all ages, even to the end of the world. Let us neither be deterred, therefore, nor fly from its instructions, because it prescribes a holiness far more complete than we shall attain, as long as we remain in the prison of the body. For it no longer exercises towards us the part of a rigorous exactor, only to be satisfied by the perfect performance of every injunction; but in this perfection, to which it exhorts us, it shows us a goal, to aim at which, during the whole of our lives, would be equally conducive to our interest and consistent with our duty; in which attempt it is happy for us if we fail not. For the whole of this life is a course, which when we have completed, the Lord will grant us to reach that goal, towards which at so great a distance our efforts are now vigorously directed.

XIV. Now, because the law, in regard to the faithful, has the force of an exhortation, not to bind their consciences with a curse, but by its frequent admonitions to arouse their indolence, and reprove their imperfection,—many persons, when they design to express this liberation from its curse, say that the law (I still speak of the moral law) is abrogated to the faithful; not that it no longer enjoins upon them that which is right, but only that it ceases to be to them what it was before, no longer terrifying and confounding their consciences, condemning and destroying them. And such an abrogation of the law is clearly taught by Paul. It appears also to have been preached by our Lord, since he would not have refuted the opinion concerning his abolishing the law, unless it had prevailed among the Jews. Now, as this opinion could not prevail without any pretext, it is probable that it proceeded from a false interpretation of his doctrine; in the same manner as almost all errors have usually taken some colour from the truth. But lest we ourselves fall into the same error, let us accurately distinguish what is abrogated in the law, and what still remains in force. When the Lord declares that he came "not to destroy the law, but to fulfil it," and that "till heaven and earth shall pass, one jot or one tittle shall in no wise pass from the law, till all be fulfilled," he sufficiently proves that his advent would detract nothing from the observance of the law. And with sufficient reason, since the express end of his advent was to heal the transgressions of it. The doctrine of the law remains, therefore, through Christ, inviolable; which by tuition, admonition, reproof, and correction, forms and prepares us for every good work.

XV. The assertions of Paul respecting the abrogation of the law evidently relate, not to the instruction itself, but to the power of binding the conscience. For the law not only teaches, but authoritatively requires, obedience to its commands. If this obedience be not yielded, and even if there be any partial deficiency of duty, it hurls the thunderbolt of its curse. For this reason the Apostle says, that "as many as are of the works of the law are under the curse; for it is written, Cursed is every one that continueth not in all things." Now, he affirms those to be "of the works of the law," who place not their righteousness in the remission of sins, by which we are released from the rigour of the law. He teaches us, therefore, that we must be released from the bondage of the law, unless we would perish in misery under it. But what bondage? the bondage of that austere and rigid exaction, which remits nothing from its strictest requirements, and permits no transgression to pass with impunity; I say, Christ, in order to redeem us from this curse, was "made a curse for us. For it is written, Cursed is every one that hangeth on a tree." In the following chapter, indeed, he tells us, that Christ was "made under the law, to redeem them that were under the law;" but in the same sense; for he immediately adds, "that we might receive the adoption of sons." What is this? that we might not be oppressed with a perpetual servitude, which would keep our consciences in continual distress with the dread of death. At the same time this truth remains for ever unshaken, that the law has sustained no diminution of its authority, but ought always to receive from us the same veneration and obedience.

XVI. The case of ceremonies, which have been abrogated, not as to their effect, but only as to their use, is very different. Their having been abolished by the advent of Christ, is so far from derogating from their sanctity, that it rather recommends and renders it more illustrious. For as they must have exhibited to the people, in ancient times, a vain spectacle, unless they had discovered the virtue of the death and resurrection of Christ, so, if they had not ceased, we should, in the present age, have been unable to discern for what purpose they were instituted. To prove, therefore, that the observance of them is not only needless, but even injurious, Paul teaches us that they were shadows, the body of which we have in Christ. We see, then, that the truth shines with greater splendour in their abolition, than if they still continued to give a distant and obscure representation of Christ, who has openly appeared. For this reason, at the death of Christ, "the veil of the temple was rent in twain from the top to the bottom;" because, according to the author of the Epistle to the Hebrews, the living and express image of the heavenly blessings, which before had been only sketched in obscure lineaments, was now clearly revealed. The same truth is conveyed in the declaration of Christ, that "the law and the prophets were until John; since that time the kingdom of God is preached." Not that the holy fathers had been destitute of that preaching which contains the hope of salvation, and of eternal life, but because they saw only at a distance, and under shadows, what we now contemplate in open day. But the reason, why it was necessary for the Church of God to ascend from those rudiments to sublimer heights, is explained by John the Baptist: "the law was given by Moses, but grace and truth came by Jesus

Christ." For although expiation of sin was truly promised in the ancient sacrifices, and the ark of the covenant was a certain pledge of the paternal favour of God, all these would have been mere shadows, if they had not been founded in the grace of Christ, where alone we may find true and eternal stability. Let us firmly maintain, then, that though the legal rites have ceased to be observed, yet their very discontinuance gives us a better knowledge of their great utility before the advent of Christ, who, abolishing the observance of them, confirmed their virtue and efficacy in his death.

XVII. The reasoning of Paul is attended with more difficulty: "And you, being dead in your sins, and the uncircumcision of your flesh, hath he quickened together with him, having forgiven you all trespasses; blotting out the hand-writing of ordinances that was against us, which was contrary to us, and took it out of the way, nailing it to his cross," &c. For it seems to extend the abolition of the law somewhat further, as though we had now no concern with its "ordinances." For they are in an error who understand it simply of the moral law, the abolition of which they, nevertheless, explain to relate to its inexorable severity, rather than to its precepts. Others, more acutely and carefully considering the words of Paul, perceive that they belong particularly to the ceremonial law; and prove that the word "ordinances" is more than once used by Paul in that signification. For he thus expresses himself to the Ephesians: "He is our peace, who hath made both one; having abolished the law of commandments contained in ordinances; for to make in himself of twain one new man." That he there speaks of the ceremonies, is very evident; for he calls the law "the middle wall of partition," by which the Jews were separated from the Gentiles. Wherefore I allow that the former commentators are justly censured by these; but even these do not appear to me clearly to explain the meaning of the Apostle. For to compare these two passages as in all respects similar, is what I by no means approve. When he designs to assure the Ephesians of their admission into fellowship with the Israelites, he informs them, that the impediment which formerly prevented it is now removed. That consisted in ceremonies. For the rites of ablutions and sacrifices, by which the Jews were consecrated to the Lord, caused a separation between them and the Gentiles. But in the Epistle to the Colossians he treats of a sublimer mystery. The controversy there relates to the Mosaic observances, to which the false Apostles were strenuously attempting to subject the Christians. But as in the Epistle to the Galatians he goes to the depth of that controversy, and reduces it to its source, so also in this place. For if in the rites you contemplate nothing but the necessity of performing them, to what purpose were they called a "hand-writing that was against us"? and almost the whole of our redemption made to consist in its being "blotted out?" Wherefore it is evident, that here is something to be considered beside the external ceremonies. And I am persuaded that I have discovered the genuine meaning, at least if that be conceded to me as a truth, which Augustine somewhere very truly asserts, and which he has even borrowed from the positive expressions of an Apostle, that in the Jewish ceremonies there was rather a confession of sins than an expiation of them. For what did they do in offering sacrifices, but confess themselves worthy of death, since they substituted victims to be slain in their stead? What were their purifications, but confessions that they were themselves impure? Thus the hand-writing both of their sin and of their impurity was frequently renewed by them; but that confession afforded no deliverance. For which reason the Apostle says that the death of Christ effected "the redemption of the transgressions that were under the first testament." The Apostle, therefore, justly denominates the ceremonies "a hand-writing against those who observe them;" because by them they publicly attested their condemnation and impurity. Nor does any objection arise from their having been also partakers of the same grace with us. For this they obtained in Christ, not in the ceremonies, which the Apostle there distinguishes from Christ; for being practised at that time after the introduction of the gospel, they obscured the glory of Christ. We find, then, that the ceremonies, considered by themselves, are beautifully and appositely called a "hand-writing that was against" the salvation of men; because they were solemn instruments testifying their guilt. When the false Apostles wished to bring the Church back to the observance of them, the Apostle deeply investigated their signification, and very justly admonished the Colossians into what circumstances they would relapse, if they should suffer themselves to be thus enslaved by them. For they would at the same time be deprived of the benefit of Christ; since, by the eternal expiation that he has once effected, he has abolished those daily observances, which could only attest their sins, but could never cancel them.

2. AN EXPOSITION OF THE MORAL LAW

Here I think it will not be foreign to our subject to introduce the ten precepts of the law, with a brief exposition of them. For this will more clearly evince what I have suggested, that the service which God has once prescribed always remains in full force; and will also furnish us with a confirmation of the second remark, that the Jews not only learned from it the nature of true piety, but when they saw their inability to observe it, were led by the fear of its sentence, though not without reluctance, to the Mediator. Now, in giving a summary of those things which are requisite to the true knowledge of God, we have shown that we can form no conceptions of his greatness, but his majesty immediately discovers itself to us, to constrain us to worship him. In the knowledge of ourselves, we have laid down this as a principal article, that being divested of all opinion of our own strength, and confidence in our own righteousness, and, on the other hand, discouraged and depressed by a consciousness of our poverty, we should learn true humility and self-dejection. The Lord accomplishes both these things in his law, where, in the first place, claiming to himself the legitimate authority to command, he calls us to revere his Divinity, and prescribes the parts of which this reverence consists; and in the next place, promulgating the rule of his righteousness, (the rectitude of which, our nature, being depraved and perverted, perpetually opposes; and from the perfection of which, our ability, through its indolence and imbecility towards that which is good, is at a great distance,) he convicts us both of impotence and of unrighteousness. Moreover, the internal law, which has before been said to be inscribed and as it were engraven on the hearts of all men, suggests to us in some measure the same things which are to be learned from the two tables. For our conscience does not permit us to sleep in perpetual insensibility, but is an internal witness and monitor of the duties we owe to God, shows us the difference between good and evil, and so accuses us when we deviate from our duty. But man, involved as he is in a cloud of errors, scarcely obtains from this law of nature the smallest idea of what worship is accepted by God; but is certainly at an immense distance from a right understanding of it. Besides, he is so elated with arrogance and ambition, and so blinded with self-love, that he cannot yet take a view of himself, and as it were retire within, that he may learn to submit and humble himself, and to confess his misery. Since it was necessary, therefore, both for our dulness and obstinacy, the Lord gave us a written law; to declare with greater certainty what in the law of nature was too obscure, and by arousing our indolence, to make a deeper impression on our understanding and memory.

II. Now, it is easy to perceive, what we are to learn from the law; namely, that God, as he is our Creator, justly sustains towards us the character of a Father and of a Lord; and that on this account we owe to him glory and reverence, love and fear. Moreover, that we are not at liberty to follow every thing to which the violence of our passions may incite us; but that we ought to be attentive to his will, and to practise nothing but what is pleasing to him. In the next place, that righteousness and rectitude are a delight, but iniquity an abomination to him; and that, therefore, unless we will with impious ingratitude rebel against our Maker, we must necessarily spend our whole lives in the practice of righteousness. For if we manifest a becoming reverence for him, only when we prefer his will to our own, it follows that there is no other legitimate worship of him, but the observance of righteousness, sanctity, and purity. Nor can we pretend to excuse ourselves by a want of ability, like insolvent debtors. For it is improper for us to measure the glory of God by our ability; for whatever may be our characters, he ever remains like himself, the friend of righteousness, the enemy of iniquity. Whatever he requires of us, since he can require nothing but what is right, we are under a natural obligation to obey; but our inability is our own fault. For if we are bound by our own passions, which are under the government of sin, so that we are not at liberty to obey our Father, there is no reason why we should plead this necessity in our defence, the criminality of which is within ourselves, and must be imputed to us.

III. When we have made such a proficiency as this by means of the instruction of the law, we ought, under the same teacher, to retire within ourselves; from which we may learn two things: First, by comparing our life with the righteousness of the law, we shall find, that we are very far from acting agreeably to the will of God, and are therefore unworthy to retain a place among his creatures, much less to be numbered among his children. Secondly, by examining our strength, we shall see, that it is not only unequal to the observance of the law, but a mere nullity. The necessary consequence of this will be a diffidence in our own strength, and an anxiety and trepidation of mind. For the conscience cannot sustain the load of iniquity, without an immediate discovery of the Divine judgment. And the Divine judgment cannot be perceived, without inspiring a dread of death. Compelled also by proofs of its impotence, it cannot avoid falling into an absolute despair of its own strength. Both these dispositions produce humility and dejection. The result of all this is, that the man terrified with the apprehension of eternal death, which he sees justly impending over him for his unrighteousness, betakes himself entirely to the Divine mercy, as to the only port of salvation; and perceiving his inability to fulfil the commands of the law, and feeling nothing but despair in himself, he implores and expects assistance from another quarter.

IV. But not contented with having conciliated a reverence for his righteousness, the Lord has also subjoined promises and threatenings, in order that our hearts might imbibe a love for him, and at the same time a hatred to iniquity. For since the eyes of our mind are too dim to be attracted with the mere beauty of virtue, our most merciful Father has been graciously pleased to allure us to the love and worship of himself by the sweetness of his rewards. He announces, therefore, that he has reserved rewards for virtue, and that the person who obeys his commandments shall not labour in vain. He proclaims, on the contrary, not only that unrighteousness is execrable in his sight, but also that it shall not escape with impunity; but that he will avenge himself on all the despisers of his majesty. And to urge us by all possible motives, he promises also the blessings of the present life, as well as eternal felicity, to the obedience of those who keep his commandments, the transgressors of which he threatens not only with present calamities, but with the torments of eternal death. For that promise, "these if a man do, he shall live in them," and this correspondent threatening, "the soul that sinneth, it shall die," undoubtedly relate to a future and endless immortality or death. Wherever we read of the Divine benevolence or wrath, the former comprehends eternal life, the latter eternal destruction. Now, of present blessings and curses, the law contains a long catalogue. The penal sanctions display the consummate purity of God, which cannot tolerate iniquity; while the promises not only manifest his perfect love of righteousness, which he cannot defraud of its reward, but likewise illustrate his wonderful goodness. For since we, with all that belongs to us, are indebted to his majesty, whatever he requires of us, he most justly demands as the payment of a debt; but the payment of a debt is not entitled to remuneration. Therefore he recedes from the strictness of his claims, when he proposes a reward to our obedience, which is not performed spontaneously, as if it were not a duty. But the effect of those promises on us has partly been mentioned already, and will hereafter more clearly appear in its proper place. Suffice it at present, if we remember and consider that the promises of the law contain no mean recommendation of righteousness, to make it more evident how much God is pleased with the observance of it; and that the penal sanctions are annexed, to render unrighteousness more execrable, lest the sinner, amidst the fascinations of sin, should forget that the judgment of the Legislator awaits him.

V. Now, since the Lord, when about to deliver a rule of perfect righteousness, referred all the parts of it to his own will, this shows that nothing is more acceptable to him than obedience. This is worthy of the most diligent observation, since the licentiousness of the human mind is so inclined to the frequent invention of various services in order to merit his favour. For this irreligious affectation of religion, which is a principle innate in the human mind, has betrayed itself in all ages, and betrays itself even in the present day; for men always take a pleasure in contriving some way of attaining righteousness, which is not agreeable to the Divine word. Hence, among those which are commonly esteemed good works, the precepts of the law hold a very contracted station, the numberless multitude of human inventions occupying almost the whole space. But what was the design of Moses, unless it was to repress such an unwarrantable license, when, after the promulgation of the law, he addressed the people in the following manner! "Observe and hear all these words which I command thee, that it may go well with thee, and with thy children after thee for ever, when thou doest that which is good and right in the sight of the Lord thy God. What thing soever I command you, observe to do it: thou shalt not add thereto, nor diminish from it." And before, when he had declared that this was their wisdom and their understanding in the sight of other nations, that they had received statutes, and judgments, and ceremonies, from the Lord, he had added, "Take heed to thyself, and keep thy soul diligently, lest thou forget the things which thine eyes have seen, and lest they depart from thy heart all the days of thy life." Foreseeing that the Israelites would not rest, but, even after the reception of the law, would labour to produce new species of righteousness, foreign from what the law requires, unless they should be rigorously restrained, God pronounces that his word comprehends the perfection of righteousness; and yet, though this ought most effectually to have prevented them, they were guilty of that very presumption which was so expressly forbidden. But what is this to us? We are certainly bound by the same declaration; for the claims of the Lord on behalf of his law, that it contains the doctrine of perfect righteousness, beyond all doubt remain perpetually the same; yet not contented with it, we are wonderfully laborious in inventing and performing other good works, one after another. The best remedy for this fault will be a constant attention to this reflection; that the law was given to us from heaven to teach us a perfect righteousness; that in it no righteousness is taught, but that which is conformable to the decrees of the Divine will; that it is therefore vain to attempt new species of works in order to merit the favour of God, whose legitimate worship consists solely in obedience, but that any pursuit of good works deviating from the law of God is an intolerable profanation of the Divine and real righteousness. There is much truth also in the observation of Augustine, who calls obedience to God sometimes the parent and guardian, and sometimes the origin of all virtues.

VI. But when we have given an exposition of the Divine law, we shall then more suitably and profitably confirm what has been already advanced concerning its office and use. Before we enter, however, on the discussion of each article separately, it will be useful to premise some things which may contribute to a general knowledge of it. First, let it be understood, that the law inculcates a conformity of life, not only to external probity, but also to internal and spiritual righteousness. Now, though none can deny this, yet very few persons pay proper attention to it. This arises from their not considering the Legislator, by whose nature we ought to estimate also the nature of the law. If a king prohibit, by an edict, adultery, murder, or theft, no man, I confess, will be liable to the penalty of such a law, who has only conceived in his mind a desire to commit adultery, murder, or theft, but has not perpetrated any of them. Because the superintendence of a mortal legislator extends only to the external conduct, and his prohibitions are not violated unless the crimes be actually committed. But God, whose eye nothing escapes, and who esteems not so much the external appearance as the purity of the heart, in the prohibition of adultery, murder, and theft, comprises a prohibition of lust, wrath, hatred, coveting what belongs to another, fraud, and every similar vice. For, being a spiritual Legislator, he addresses himself to the soul as much as to the body. Now, the murder of the soul is wrath and hatred; the theft of the soul is evil concupiscence and avarice; the adultery of the soul is lust. But it will be said, that human laws also relate to designs and intentions, and not to fortuitous events. This I grant; but they relate to such designs and intentions as have been manifested in outward actions. They examine and consider with what intention every act has been performed; but do not scrutinize the secret thoughts. Human laws therefore are satisfied, when a man abstains from external transgression. But, on the contrary, the Divine law being given to our minds, the proper regulation of them is the principal requisite to a righteous observance of it. But men in general, even while they resolutely dissemble their contempt of the law, dispose their eyes, their feet, their hands, and all the parts of their body, to some kind of observance of it, while at the same time their hearts are entirely alienated from all obedience to it, and they suppose that they have discharged their duty, if they have concealed from man what they practise in the sight of God. They hear the commands, Thou shalt not kill, Thou shalt not commit adultery, Thou shalt not steal. They draw not the sword to commit murder; they never associate with harlots; they lay no violent hands on the property of others. All these things thus far are well; but in their whole souls they breathe after murders, they kindle into lust, they look with dishonest eyes on the property of others, and in their cupidity they devour it. Now, then, they are destitute of the principal requisite of the law. Whence arises such gross stupidity, but from discarding the Legislator, and accommodating a righteousness to their own inclination? These persons Paul strongly opposes, when he affirms that "the law is spiritual;" signifying that it requires not only the obedience of the soul, the understanding, and the will, but even an angelic purity, which, being cleansed from all the pollution of the flesh, may savour entirely of the Spirit.

VII. When we say that this is the sense of the law, we are not introducing a novel interpretation of our own, but following Christ, who is the best interpreter of it. For the people having imbibed from the Pharisees the corrupt opinion, that he, who has perpetrated no external act of disobedience to the law, is an observer of the law, he confutes this very dangerous error, and pronounces an unchaste look at a woman to be adultery; he declares them to be murderers, who hate a brother; he makes them "in danger of the judgment," who have only conceived resentment in their hearts; them "in danger of the council," who in murmuring or quarrelling have discovered any sign of an angry mind; and them "in danger of hell fire," who with opprobrious and slanderous language have broken forth into open rage. Persons who have not perceived these things, have pretended that Christ was another Moses, the giver of an evangelical law, which supplied the deficiencies of the law of Moses. Whence that common maxim, concerning the perfection of the evangelical law, that it is far superior to the old law—a maxim in many respects very pernicious. For when we introduce a summary of the commandments, it will appear from Moses himself what an indignity this fixes on the Divine law. It certainly insinuates that all the sanctity of the fathers under the Old Testament, was not very remote from hypocrisy, and draws us aside from that one perpetual rule of righteousness. But there is not the least difficulty in the confutation of this error; for they have supposed that Christ made additions to the law, whereas he only restored it to its genuine purity, by clearing it from the obscurities and blemishes which it had contracted from the falsehoods and the leaven of the Pharisees.

VIII. It must be observed, in the second place, that the commands and prohibitions always imply more than the words express; but this must be so restricted, that we may not make it a Lesbian rule, by the assistance of which the Scripture may be licentiously perverted, and any sense be extorted at pleasure from any passage. For some people, by this immoderate and excursive liberty, cause one person to despise the authority of the law, and another to despair of understanding it. Therefore, if it be possible, we must find some way that may lead us by a straight and steady course to the will of God. We must inquire, I say, how far our interpretation ought to exceed the limits of the expressions; that it may evidently appear, not to be an appendix of human glosses annexed to the Divine law, but a faithful explanation of the pure and genuine sense of the legislator. Indeed, in all the commandments, the figure synecdoche, by which a part is expressed instead of the whole, is so conspicuous, that he may justly be the object of ridicule, who would restrict the sense of the law within the narrow limits of the words. It is plain, then, that a sober exposition of the law goes beyond the words of it; but how far, remains doubtful, unless some rule be laid down. The best rule, then, I conceive will be, that the exposition be directed to the design of the precept; that in regard to every precept it should be considered for what end it was given. For example, every precept is either imperative or prohibitory. The true meaning of both these kinds of precepts will immediately occur to us, if we consider the design or the end of them; as the end of the fifth commandment is, that honour may be given to them to whom God assigns it. The substance of this precept, then, is, that it is right, and pleasing to God, that we should honour those on whom he has conferred any excellence, and that contemptuous and contumacious conduct towards them is an abomination to him. The design of the first commandment is, that God alone may be worshipped. The substance of this precept, then, will be, that true piety, that is, the worship of his majesty, is pleasing to God, and that he abominates impiety. Thus in every commandment we should first examine the subject of it; in the next place we should inquire the end of it, till we discover what the Legislator really declares in it to be either pleasing or displeasing to him. Lastly, we must draw an argument from this commandment to the opposite of it, in this manner:—If this please God, the contrary must displease him; if this displease him, the contrary must please him; if he enjoin this, he forbids the contrary; if he forbid this, he enjoins the contrary.

IX. What we now rather obscurely hint at, will be fully and practically elucidated in our exposition of the commandments. Wherefore it is sufficient to have suggested it; only the last position, which otherwise might not be understood, or, if understood, might seem unreasonable, requires to be briefly established by suitable proof. It needs no proof, that an injunction of any thing good is a prohibition of the opposite evil; for every man will concede it. And common sense will easily admit, that a prohibition of crimes is a command to practise the contrary duties. It is commonly considered as a commendation of virtues, when censure is passed on the opposite vices. But we require somewhat more than is commonly intended by those forms of expression. For men generally understand the virtue which is opposite to any vice to be an abstinence from that vice; but we affirm that it goes further, even to the actual performance of the opposite duty. Therefore, in this precept, "Thou shalt not kill," the common sense of mankind will perceive nothing more than that we ought to abstain from all acts of injury to others, and from all desire to commit any such acts. I maintain that it also implies, that we should do every thing that we possibly can towards the preservation of the life of our neighbour. And not to speak without reason, I prove it in the following manner: God forbids us to injure the safety of our brother, because he wishes his life to be dear and precious to us: he therefore at the same time requires of us all those offices of love which may contribute to the preservation of it. Thus we perceive, that the end of the precept will always discover to us whatever it enjoins or forbids us to do.

X. Many reasons are frequently given, why God has, as it were, in incomplete precepts, rather partially intimated his will than positively expressed it; but the reason which affords me more satisfaction than all others is the following. Because the flesh always endeavours to extenuate, and by specious pretexts to conceal the turpitude of sin, unless it be exceedingly palpable, he has proposed, by way of example, in every kind of transgression, that which is most atrocious and detestable, and the mention of which inspires us with horror, in order that our minds might be impressed with the greater detestation of every sin. This often deceives us in forming an opinion of vices; if they be private, we extenuate them. The Lord destroys these subterfuges, when he accustoms us to refer the whole multitude of vices to these general heads, which best represent the abominable nature of every species of transgressions. For example, anger and hatred are not supposed to be such execrable crimes when they are mentioned under their own proper appellations; but when they are forbidden to us under the name of murder, we have a clearer perception how abominable they are in the view of God, by whose word they are classed under such a flagitious and horrible species of crimes; and being influenced by his judgment, we accustom ourselves more seriously to consider the atrociousness of those offences which we previously accounted trivial.

XI. In the third place, let it be considered, what is intended by the division of the Divine law into two tables; the frequent and solemn mention of which all wise men will judge not to be without some particular design. And we have a reason at hand, which removes all ambiguity on this subject. For God has divided his law into two parts, which comprise the perfection of righteousness, so that he has assigned the first part to the duties of religion, which peculiarly belongs to the worship of his majesty, and the second to those duties of charity, which respect men. The first foundation of righteousness is certainly the worship of God; and if this be destroyed, all the other branches of righteousness, like the parts of a disjointed and falling edifice, are torn asunder and scattered. For what kind of righteousness will you pretend to, because you refrain from harassing men by acts of theft and rapine, if at the same time you atrociously and sacrilegiously defraud the majesty of God of the glory which is due to him?—because you do not pollute your body with fornication, if you blasphemously profane the sacred name of God?—because you murder no man, if you strive to destroy and extinguish all memory of God? It is in vain, therefore, to boast of righteousness without religion; as well might the trunk of a body be exhibited as a beautiful object, after the head has been cut off. Nor is religion only the head of righteousness, but the very soul of it, constituting all its life and vigour; for without the fear of God, men preserve no equity and love among themselves. We therefore call the worship of God the principle and foundation of righteousness, because, if that be wanting, whatever equity, continence, and temperance men may practise among themselves, it is all vain and frivolous in the sight of God. We assert also that it is the source and soul of righteousness; because men are taught by it to live temperately and justly with one another, if they venerate God as the judge of right and wrong. In the first table, therefore, he instructs us in piety and the proper duties of religion, in which his majesty is to be worshipped; in the second he prescribes the duties which the fear of his name should excite us to practise in society. For this reason our Lord, as the evangelists inform us, summarily comprised the whole law in two principal points—that we love God with all our heart, with all our soul, and with all our strength; and that we love our neighbour as ourselves. Of the two parts in which he comprehends the whole law, we see how he directs one towards God, and assigns the other to men.

XII. But, although the whole law is contained in these two principal points, yet our God, in order to remove every pretext of excuse, has been pleased in the ten commandments more diffusely and explicitly to declare, as well those things which relate to our honour, love, and fear of him, as those which pertain to that charity, which he commands us for his sake to exercise towards men. Nor is it a useless study to examine into the division of the commandments; provided you remember it is a subject of such a nature, that every man ought to be at liberty to judge of it, and that we ought not contentiously to oppose any who may differ from us respecting it. But we are under a necessity of touching on this topic, lest the reader should despise or wonder at the division that we shall adopt, as a novel invention. That the law is divided into ten precepts, is beyond all controversy, being frequently established by the authority of God himself. The question, therefore, is not concerning the number of the precepts, but concerning the manner of dividing them. Those who divide them, so as to assign three precepts to the first table, and leave the remaining seven to the second, expunge from the number the precept concerning images, or at least conceal it under the first; whereas it is undoubtedly delivered by the Lord as a distinct commandment. But the tenth, against coveting the property of our neighbour, they improperly divide into two. We shall see presently that such a method of division was unknown in purer ages. Others reckon with us four articles in the first table; but the first commandment they consider as a simple promise, without a precept. Now, I understand the "ten words" mentioned by Moses to be ten precepts; and I think I see that number disposed in the most beautiful order. And therefore, unless I am convinced by clear argument, leaving them in possession of their opinion, I shall follow what appears to me to be preferable; that is, that what they make the first precept is a preface to the whole law; that it is followed by the precepts, four belonging to the first table and six to the second, in the order in which they will now be recited. Origen has mentioned this division as if it were universally received in his time without any controversy. Augustine also coincides with us; for in enumerating them to Boniface, he observes this order: That God alone be religiously worshipped; that no adoration be paid to an idol; that the name of the Lord be not taken in vain. He had before spoken separately of the shadowy precept of the sabbath. It is true, that in another passage he expresses his approbation of the former division, but for a most trivial reason; namely, that if the first table be digested into three precepts, the trinal number will be a more conspicuous exhibition of the mystery of the Trinity. In the same place, however, he does not conceal that in other respects he prefers our division. Beside these writers, the author of the unfinished treatise on Matthew is of the same opinion with us. Josephus, doubtless according to the common opinion of his time, assigns five precepts to each table. This is repugnant to reason, because it confounds the distinction between religion and charity; and is also refuted by the authority of our Lord, who in Matthew places the precept concerning honour to parents in the second table. Now let us hear God himself speaking in his own words.

THE FIRST COMMANDMENT.

I am the Lord thy God, which have brought thee out of the land of Egypt, out of the house of bondage. Thou shalt have no other gods before me.

XIII. Whether you make the first sentence a part of the first commandment, or read it separately, is a matter of indifference to me, provided you allow it to be a preface to the whole law. The first object of attention in making laws is to guard against their being abrogated by contempt. Therefore God in the first place provides, that the majesty of the law, which he is about to deliver, may never fall into contempt; and to sanction it he uses a threefold argument. He asserts his authority and right of giving commands, and thereby lays his chosen people under a necessity of obeying them. He exhibits a promise of grace, to allure them by its charms to the pursuit of holiness. He reminds the Israelites of his favour, to convict them of ingratitude if they do not conduct themselves in a manner correspondent to his goodness. The name Lord, or Jehovah, designates his authority and legitimate dominion. For if all things be of him, and if in him all things consist, it is reasonable that all things be referred to him, agreeably to the observation of Paul. Therefore by this word alone we are brought into complete subjection to the power of the Divine majesty; for it would be monstrous for us to desire to remove ourselves from his jurisdiction, out of whom we cannot exist.

XIV. After having shown that he has a right to command, and that obedience is his just due,—that he may not appear to constrain us by necessity alone, he sweetly allures us by pronouncing himself the God of the Church. For the expression implies the mutual relation which is contained in that promise, "I will be their God, and they shall be my people." Whence Christ proves the immortality of Abraham, Isaac, and Jacob, from the declaration of the Lord, that he is their God. Wherefore it is the same as if he had said, I have chosen you as my people, not only to bless you in the present life, but to bestow upon you abundant felicity in the life to come. The design of this favour is remarked in various places in the law; for when the Lord in mercy condescends to number us among the society of his people, "He chooseth us," says Moses, "to be a peculiar people unto himself, a holy people, to keep his commandments." Hence that exhortation, "Ye shall be holy, for I am holy." Now, from these two considerations is derived the remonstrance of the Lord by the Prophet: "A son honoureth his father, and a servant his master; if then I be a father, where is mine honour? and if I be a master, where is my fear?"

XV. Next follows a recital of his kindness, which ought to produce a most powerful effect upon our minds, in proportion to the detestable guilt of ingratitude, even among men. He reminded the Israelites, indeed, of a favour which they had recently experienced, but which, on account of its magnitude and concomitant miracles, being worthy of everlasting remembrance, might also have an influence on succeeding generations. Besides, it was particularly suitable to the present occasion, when the law was about to be published; for the Lord suggests that they were liberated from a miserable slavery in order that they might serve the author of their liberty with a promptitude of reverence and obedience. To retain us in the true and exclusive worship of himself, he generally distinguishes himself by certain epithets, by which he discriminates his sacred name from all idols and fictitious deities. For, as I have before observed, such is our proneness to vanity and presumption, that as soon as God is mentioned, our mind is unable to guard itself from falling into some vain imagination. Therefore, when God intends to apply a remedy to this evil, he adorns his majesty with certain titles, and thus circumscribes us with barriers, that we may not run into various follies, and presumptuously invent to ourselves some new deity, discarding the living God, and setting up an idol in his stead. For this reason the Prophets, whenever they intend a proper designation of him, invest him, and as it were surround him, with those characters under which he had manifested himself to the people of Israel. Yet, when he is called "the God of Abraham," or "the God of Israel," when he is said to reside "between the cherubim," "in the temple," "at Jerusalem," these and similar forms of expression do not confine him to one place, or to one nation; they are only used to fix the thoughts of the pious on that God, who, in the covenant which he has made with Israel, has given such a representation of himself, that it is not proper to deviate in the smallest instance from such a model. Nevertheless, let it be concluded, that the deliverance of the Jews is mentioned to induce them to devote themselves with more alacrity to the service of God, who justly claims a right to their obedience. But, that we may not suppose this to have no relation to us, it behoves us to consider, that the servitude of Israel in Egypt was a type of the spiritual captivity, in which we are all detained, till our celestial Deliverer extricates us by the power of his arm, and introduces us into the kingdom of liberty. As formerly, therefore, when he designed to restore the dispersed Israelites to the worship of his name, he rescued them from the intolerable tyranny of Pharaoh, by which they were oppressed, so now he delivers all those, whose God he declares himself to be, from the fatal dominion of Satan, which was represented by that corporeal captivity. Wherefore there is no one, whose mind ought not to be excited to listen to the law, which he is informed came from the King of kings; from whom as all creatures derive their origin, so it is reasonable that they should regard him as their end in all things. Every man, I say, ought to welcome the Legislator; to observe whose commands he is taught that he is particularly chosen; from whose benignity he expects an abundance of temporal blessings, and a life of immortality and glory; by whose wonderful power and mercy he knows himself to be delivered from the jaws of death.

XVI. Having firmly established the authority of his law, he publishes the first commandment, "That we should have no other gods before him." The end of this precept is, that God chooses to have the sole preëminence, and to enjoy undiminished his authority among his people. To produce this end, he enjoins us to keep at a distance from all impiety and superstition, by which we should either diminish or obscure the glory of his Deity; and for the same reason he directs us to worship and adore him in the exercise of true piety. The simplicity of the language almost expresses this; for we cannot "have" God without at the same time comprising all that belongs to him. Therefore, when he forbids us to "have" any other gods, he implies, that we must not transfer to another what belongs to him. But although the duties we owe to God are innumerable, yet they may not improperly be classed under four general heads—adoration, a necessary branch of which is the spiritual obedience of the conscience; trust; invocation; and thanksgiving. By adoration I mean the reverence and worship which he receives from every one of us who has submitted to his majesty. Wherefore it is not without reason that I make it partly to consist in a subjection of our consciences to his law; [for it is a spiritual homage which is rendered to him, as to a sovereign King possessed of all power over our souls.] Trust is a secure dependence on him arising from a knowledge of his perfections; when ascribing to him all wisdom, righteousness, power, truth, and goodness, we esteem ourselves happy only in communications from him. Invocation is the application of our minds, under every pressure of necessity, resorting to his fidelity, faithfulness, and assistance, as its only defence. Thanksgiving is gratitude, which ascribes to him the praise of all blessings. As the Lord permits no portion of these duties to be transferred to another, so he commands them to be wholly given to himself. Nor will it be sufficient for you to refrain from worshipping any other god, unless you also refrain from imitating certain nefarious despisers, who take the compendious method of treating all religions with contempt. But the observance of this precept must be preceded by true religion, leading our minds to the living God; that being endued with the knowledge of him, they may aspire to admire, fear, and worship his majesty, to receive his communication of blessings, to request his aid upon all occasions, to acknowledge and celebrate the magnificence of his works, as the sole end in all the actions of our lives. We must also beware of corrupt superstition, by which those whose minds are diverted from the true God, are carried about after various deities. Therefore, if we be contented with one God, let us remember what has before been observed, that all fictitious deities must be driven far away, and that we must not divide that worship which he claims exclusively to himself. For it is criminal to detract even the smallest portion from his glory; he must be left in possession of all that belongs to him. The following clause, "before me," aggravates the atrociousness of the offence; for God is provoked to jealousy whenever we substitute the figments of our own minds instead of him; just as an immodest woman, by openly introducing an adulterer into the presence of her husband, would inflame his mind with the greater resentment. When God, therefore, by the presence of his power and grace, gave a proof of his regard to the people whom he had chosen,—in order the more forcibly to deter them from the crime of rebellion against him, he warns them of the impossibility of introducing new deities without his being a witness and spectator of the sacrilege. For this presumption rises to the highest degree of impiety, when man imagines that he can elude the observation of God in his acts of rebellion. God, on the contrary, proclaims, that whatever we devise, whatever we attempt, whatever we perform, is present to his view. Our conscience must therefore be pure even from the most latent thoughts of apostasy, if we wish our religion to obtain the approbation of the Lord. For he requires from us the glory due to his Divinity undiminished and uncorrupted, not only in external confession, but in his own eyes, which penetrate the inmost recesses of our hearts.

THE SECOND COMMANDMENT.

Thou shalt not make unto thee any graven image, or any likeness of any thing that is in heaven above, or that is in the earth beneath, or that is in the water under the earth. Thou shalt not bow down thyself to them, nor serve them.

XVII. As in the preceding commandment the Lord has declared himself to be the one God, besides whom no other deities ought to be imagined or worshipped, so in this he more clearly reveals his nature, and the kind of worship with which he ought to be honoured, that we may not dare to form any carnal conceptions of him. The end, therefore, of this precept is, that he will not have his legitimate worship profaned with superstitious rites. Wherefore, in a word, he calls us off, and wholly abstracts us from carnal observances, which our foolish minds are accustomed to devise, when they conceive of God according to the grossness of their own apprehensions; and therefore he calls us to the service which rightfully belongs to him; that is, the spiritual worship which he has instituted. He marks what is the grossest transgression of this kind; that is, external idolatry. And this precept consists of two parts. The first restrains us from licentiously daring to make God, who is incomprehensible, the subject of our senses, or to represent him under any visible form. The second prohibits us from paying religious adoration to any images. He likewise briefly enumerates all the forms, in which he used to be represented by profane and superstitious nations. By those things which are in heaven, he means the sun, the moon, and the other stars, and perhaps birds; as, when he explains his meaning in the fourth chapter of Deuteronomy, he mentions birds as well as the stars. This I should not have remarked, had I not known some persons injudiciously refer this clause to angels. I omit the other particulars, as needing no explanation. And in the first book we have already sufficiently proved that whatever visible representations of God are invented by man, are diametrically opposite to his nature; and that, therefore, as soon as ever idols are introduced, true religion is immediately corrupted and adulterated.

XVIII. The penal sanction which is annexed ought to have no small influence in arousing us from our lethargy. He thus threatens:

For I the Lord thy God am a jealous God, visiting the iniquity of the fathers upon the children unto the third and fourth generation of them that hate me; and showing mercy unto thousands of them that love me, and keep my commandments.

This is equivalent to a declaration that it is to him alone that we ought to adhere. And to urge us to it, he announces his power, which he permits none with impunity to despise or undervalue. For the Hebrew word El, which is here used for God, is expressive of strength. In the second place, he calls himself "a jealous God," who can bear no rival. Thirdly, he declares that he will avenge his majesty and glory on those who transfer it to creatures or to graven images; and that not with the transient punishment of the original transgressors only, but of their posterity to the third and fourth generation; that is, of those who shall imitate the impiety of their fathers; as he also permanently displays his mercy and goodness, through a long line of posterity, to those who love him and keep his law. It is very common for God to assume the character of a husband to us; for the union, in which he connects us with himself, when he receives us into the bosom of his Church, bears a resemblance to the sacred conjugal relation, which requires to be supported by mutual fidelity. As he performs towards us all the duties of a true and faithful husband, so he demands from us the reciprocal duties of conjugal love and chastity; that is, that we do not prostitute our souls to Satan, to lust, and to the impurity of the carnal appetites. Wherefore, when he reproves the apostasy of the Jews, he complains that they had discarded chastity, and were polluted with adulteries. Therefore, as a husband, in proportion to the superiority of his purity and chastity, is the more grievously incensed, if he perceive the affection of his wife inclining to a rival, so the Lord, who has in truth espoused us to himself, declares that he feels the most ardent jealousy, whenever we neglect the sacred purity of his conjugal relation to us, and defile ourselves with criminal lusts, but especially when we transfer to any other, or adulterate with any superstition, the worship of his majesty, which ought to be preserved in the most consummate perfection; since by such conduct we not only violate the faith pledged in our nuptials, but even pollute our souls with spiritual adultery.

XIX. Let us inquire what he intends by his threatening to "visit the iniquity of the fathers upon the children to the third and fourth generation." For besides that it is inconsistent with the equity of the Divine justice to inflict upon an innocent person the punishment due to the offences of another, God himself declares that "the son shall not bear the iniquity of the father." But this expression is repeated more than once, concerning a deferring to future generations of the punishments of crimes committed by their ancestors. For Moses frequently speaks of "the Lord visiting the iniquity of the fathers upon the children unto the third and fourth generation." In like manner Jeremiah: "Thou showest loving-kindness unto thousands, and recompensest the iniquity of the fathers into the bosom of their children after them." Some, who labour very hard to solve this difficulty, are of opinion that its meaning is to be confined to temporal punishments; which if children sustain through the sins of their parents, there is nothing absurd in it; because they frequently conduce to the salvation of those on whom they are inflicted. This is certainly true. For Isaiah denounced to Hezekiah, that on account of the sin which he had committed, his sons should be despoiled of the kingdom and carried away into exile. The families of Pharaoh and Abimelech are afflicted on account of the injury sustained by Abraham. But when this is adduced as a solution of these questions, it is rather an evasion of it, than a proper explanation. For in this and in similar places the Lord threatens a punishment too great to be terminated by the limits of the present life. It must therefore be understood as a declaration that the curse of the Lord righteously rests, not only on the person of an impious man, but also on his whole family. Where it has rested, what can be expected, but that the father, being destitute of the Spirit of God, will lead a most flagitious life; and that the son, experiencing, in consequence of the iniquity of his father, a similar dereliction by the Lord, will pursue the same path to perdition; and that the grandson and the great grandson, the execrable posterity of detestable men, will run headlong after them down the same precipice of destruction?

XX. First let us inquire, whether such punishment be inconsistent with the Divine justice. If the whole nature of man be worthy of condemnation, we know that destruction awaits those who are not favoured by the Lord with the communication of his grace.

Nevertheless, they perish through their own iniquity, and not through the unjust hatred of God. Nor is there any room left for expostulation, why they are not assisted by Divine grace to obtain salvation as well as others. Since it is a punishment, therefore, inflicted on the impious and flagitious, in consequence of their transgressions, that their families remain destitute of Divine grace for many generations, who can bring any accusation against God for this most righteous instance of his vengeance? But it will be said, the Lord declares, on the contrary, that the punishment of the sin of the father shall not be transferred to the son. Observe the subject that is treated of in that place. The Israelites, after they had been long harassed by numerous and unceasing calamities, began to use this proverb, "The fathers have eaten sour grapes, and the children's teeth are set on edge;" by which they insinuated, that sins had been committed by their parents, the punishment of which was inflicted on them who were otherwise righteous and innocent, more through the implacable wrath of God, than through a just severity. The Prophet announces to them that this is not the case, but that they are punished for their own transgressions, and that it is incompatible with the Divine justice to punish a righteous son for the iniquity of a wicked father. Nor is this to be found in the penal sanction now under consideration. For if the visitation, of which we are treating, be fulfilled, when God removes from the family of the impious his grace, the light of his truth, and the other means of salvation, the very circumstance of children blinded and abandoned by him being found treading in the footsteps of their fathers, is an instance of their bearing the curse in consequence of the crimes of their parents. But their being the subjects of temporal miseries, and at length of eternal perdition, are punishments from the righteous judgment of God, not for the sins of others, but on account of their own iniquity.

XXI. On the other hand, God gives a promise to extend his mercy to a thousand generations; which also frequently occurs in the Scripture, and is inserted in the solemn covenant with the Church: "I will be a God unto thee, and to thy seed after thee." In allusion to this, Solomon says, that "the children of the just man are blessed after him;" not only as the effect of a religious education, which is of no small importance, but also in consequence of the blessing promised in the covenant, that the grace of God shall perpetually remain in the families of the pious. This is a source of peculiar consolation to the faithful, but to the impious of great terror; for if, even after death, the memory of righteousness and iniquity has so much influence with God, that the curse of the one and the blessing of the other will redound to posterity, much more will it remain on the persons of the actors themselves. Now, it is no objection to our argument, that the descendants of the impious sometimes grow better, while those of the faithful degenerate; since the Legislator never intended to establish in this case such an invariable rule, as would derogate from his own free choice. For it is sufficient for the consolation of the righteous and the terror of the sinner, that the denunciation is not vain or inefficacious, although it be not always executed. For as the temporal punishments inflicted on a few wicked men are testimonies of the Divine wrath against sin, and of the judgment that will hereafter be pronounced on all sinners, though many escape with impunity even to the end of their lives, so, when the Lord exhibits one example of this blessing, in manifesting his mercy and goodness to the son for the sake of his father, he affords a proof of his constant and perpetual favour to his worshippers; and when, in any one instance, he pursues the iniquity of the father in the son, he shows what a judgment awaits all the reprobate on account of their own transgressions; the certainty of which was what he principally designed in this passage. He also gives us a cursory intimation of the greatness of his mercy, which he extends to a thousand generations, while he has assigned only four generations to his vengeance.

THE THIRD COMMANDMENT.

Thou shalt not take the name of the Lord thy God in vain.

XXII. The end of this precept is, that the Lord will have the majesty of his name to be held inviolably sacred by us. The substance of the command therefore is, that we ought not to profane that name by a contemptuous or irreverent use of it. This prohibition necessarily implies an injunction, that we studiously and carefully treat it with religious veneration. Therefore it becomes us to regulate our thoughts and words in such a manner that we may not think or speak any thing concerning God and his mysteries, but with the greatest sobriety and reverence; that in meditating on his works we may form no opinion that is dishonourable to him. These three things, I say, we ought most carefully to observe—first, that whatever we think, and whatever we say of him, should savour of his excellence, correspond to the sacred sublimity of his name, and tend to the exaltation of his magnificence. Secondly, we should not rashly and preposterously abuse his holy word and adorable mysteries to the purposes of ambition, of avarice, or of amusement; but as they bear an impression of the dignity of his name, they should always receive from us the honour and esteem which belong to them. Lastly, we should not injure his works by obloquy or detraction, as some miserable mortals are accustomed to do; but whenever we mention any thing done by him, we should celebrate it with encomiums of wisdom, justice, and goodness. This is "sanctifying" the name of God. In every other case, it is violated by a vain and criminal abuse, because it is carried beyond the limits of that legitimate use, to which alone it is consecrated; and though no other consequence ensue, it is deprived of its dignity, and by degrees rendered contemptible. But if it be so criminal thus rashly and unseasonably to introduce the name of God on every occasion, much more so must it be to apply it to such nefarious uses as they do, who make it subservient to the superstitions of necromancy, to horrible imprecations, to unlawful exorcisms, and to other impious incantations. But an oath is the thing principally contemplated in the command, as the most detestable instance of the perverse abuse of the Divine name; and this is done to inspire us with the greater horror of every species of profanation of it. That this precept relates to the worship of God and the reverence of his name, and not to the equity that ought to be observed among mankind, appears from this—that the subsequent condemnation, in the second table, of perjury and false witness, by which society is injured, would be a needless repetition, if the present precept related to a civil duty. Besides, the division of the law requires this; for, as we have already observed, it is not in vain that God has distributed the law into two tables. Whence we conclude, that in this command he vindicates his just claims, and guards the sanctity of his name, but does not teach the duties which men owe to each other.

XXIII. In the first place, we have to explain what an oath is. It consists in calling upon God as a witness, to confirm the truth of any declaration that we make. For execrations, which contain manifest reproaches against God, are not worthy to be mentioned among oaths. That such an attestation, when rightly performed, is a species of Divine worship, is evident from many places of Scripture; as when Isaiah prophesies of the vocation of the Assyrians and Egyptians to participate in the covenant with Israel.

"They shall speak," says he, "the language of Canaan, and swear to the Lord of hosts." By "swearing to the Lord" here is intended making a profession of religion. Again, when he speaks of the extension of his kingdom: "He who blesseth himself in the earth shall bless himself in the God of truth; and he that sweareth in the earth shall swear by the God of truth." Jeremiah says, "If they will diligently learn the ways of my people, to swear by my name, The Lord liveth; as they taught my people to swear by Baal, then shall they be built in the midst of my people." And we are justly said to profess our religion to the Lord, when we invoke his name to bear witness to us. For thereby we confess that he is truth itself, eternal and immutable; whom we call not only as a witness of the truth, excelling all others, but also as the only defender of it, who is able to bring to light things which are concealed, and in a word, as the searcher of all hearts. For where human testimonies are wanting, we resort for refuge to the testimony of God; and particularly when any thing is to be affirmed, which is hidden in the conscience. For which reason the Lord is extremely angry with them who swear by strange gods, and interprets that species of swearing as a proof of manifest defection from him. "Thy children have forsaken me, and sworn by them that are no gods." And he declares the atrociousness of this crime by his denunciation of punishment: "I will cut off them that swear by the Lord, and that swear by Malcham."

XXIV. Now, since we understand it to be the will of the Lord, that we should reverence his name in our oaths, we ought to use so much the more caution, lest, instead of reverence, they betray dishonour or contempt of it. It is no trifling insult to him, when perjury is committed in his name; and therefore the law calls it a profanation. But what remains to the Lord, when he is despoiled of his truth? he will then cease to be God. But he is certainly despoiled of it, when he is made an abettor and approver of a falsehood. Wherefore, when Joshua would induce Achan to a confession of the truth, he says, "My son, give, I pray thee, glory to the Lord God of Israel;" implying in this that the Lord is grievously dishonoured, if perjury be committed in his name. Nor is this strange; for in such a case we do all that is in our power to brand his sacred name with a falsehood. And that this form of expression was customary among the Jews, whenever any man was called to take an oath, appears from a similar adjuration used by the Pharisees in the Gospel of John. To this caution we are accustomed by the forms of oaths which are used in the Scriptures: "The Lord liveth;" "God do so and more also to me;" "I call God for a record upon my soul;" which imply, that we cannot invoke God to be a witness to our declarations, without imprecating his vengeance upon us if we be guilty of perjury.

XXV. The name of God is rendered vile and contemptible, when it is used in unnecessarily swearing even to what is true; for in this instance also it is taken in vain. Wherefore it will not be sufficient to abstain from perjury; unless we also remember, that swearing is permitted and appointed, not for the sake of our pleasure or caprice, but from necessity; and that the lawful use of it, therefore, is transgressed by those who apply it to cases where it is not necessary. Now, no other necessity can be pretended, but when we want to serve either religion or charity. This crime, in the present day, is carried to a very great extent; and it is so much the more intolerable, since by its frequency it has ceased to be considered as a crime, though before the Divine tribunal it is deemed no trivial offence. For the name of God is universally profaned without concern in trifling conversations; and it is not considered as sinful, because this presumptuous wickedness has been so long practised with impunity. But the Divine command remains valid; the sanction remains firm; and a future day will witness the completion of that part of it which denounces a particular punishment against those who take his name in vain. This precept is violated also in another way. If in our oaths we substitute the servants of God in the place of God himself, we are guilty of manifest impiety; because we thereby transfer to them the glory due to the Deity. Nor is it without reason, that God, by a special command, enjoins us to swear by his name, and by a special prohibition interdicts us from swearing by any strange gods. And the Apostle evidently attests the same, when he says, that "men swear by the greater, but that God, because he could swear by no greater, sware by himself."

XXVI. The Anabaptists, not satisfied with this limitation of oaths, condemn all oaths without exception; because the prohibition of Christ is general: "I say unto you, Swear not at all. But let your communication be, Yea, yea; Nay, nay: for whatsoever is more than these cometh of evil." But by this mode of interpretation they set Christ in opposition to the Father, as though he descended into this world to abrogate the Father's decrees. For in the law the eternal God not only permits an oath, as a lawful thing, which would be sufficient to justify the use of it, but in cases of necessity commands it. Now, Christ asserts, that "he and his Father are one," that "he acts only according to the commands of the Father," that "his doctrine is not of himself," &c. What then? Will they make God to contradict himself, by prohibiting and condemning in our conduct that which he has before approved and enjoined? But as the words of Christ involve some difficulty, let us enter on a brief examination of them. Here we shall never arrive at the truth, unless we attend to the design of Christ, and advert to the subject of which he is there treating. His design is not to relax or to restrict the law, but to reduce it to its true and genuine meaning, which had been very much corrupted by the false comments of the scribes and Pharisees. If we bear this in our minds, we shall not be of opinion that Christ condemned all oaths, but only those which transgress the rule of the law. It appears to have been the custom of the people at that time to avoid nothing but perjuries; whereas the law forbids not only perjuries, but likewise all vain and superfluous oaths. Our Lord, therefore, that infallible expositor of the law, apprizes them that it is sinful, not only to perjure themselves, but even to swear. To swear in what manner? In vain. But the oaths which are sanctioned in the law he leaves without any objection. They consider themselves as urging a very powerful argument, when they violently insist on the particle at all; which, nevertheless, refers not to the word swear, but to the forms of oaths that are there subjoined. For the error there condemned consisted, partly, in a supposition that in swearing by heaven and earth, there was no interference with the name of God. Therefore, after the principal instance of transgression, the Lord goes on to destroy all their subterfuges, that they may not imagine themselves to have escaped by suppressing the name of God, and calling heaven and earth to witness for them. For here, by the way, it must be remarked, that men indirectly swear by God, though his name is not expressed; as when they swear by the light of life, by the bread which they eat, by their baptism, or by any other blessings which they have received from the Divine munificence. Nor does Christ in that place prohibit them from swearing by heaven, and earth, and Jerusalem, in order to correct superstition, as some falsely imagine; but rather to confute the sophistical subtlety of persons who thought there was no crime in the foolish use of indirect oaths, as though they were not chargeable with profaning the sacred name of God, which is engraven, however, on all his benefits. But the case is different, where any mortal man, or one that is dead, or an angel, is substituted in the place of God; as, among idolatrous nations, adulation invented that odious form of swearing by the life or genius of a king; because in such cases the deification of a creature obscures and diminishes the glory of the only true God. But when we mean nothing but to derive a confirmation to our assertions from the sacred name of God, although it be done in an indirect manner, yet all such frivolous oaths are offensive to his majesty. Christ deprives this licentious practice of every vain excuse, by his prohibition of swearing at all. James also aims at the same point, where he uses the language of Christ, which I have cited; because this presumption has always been prevalent in the world, notwithstanding it is a profanation of the name of God. For if you refer the particle at all to the substance of swearing, as though every oath, without exception, were unlawful, what means the explanation which is immediately annexed, "Neither by heaven, neither by earth," &c., language evidently used in refutation of those cavils, which the Jews considered as furnishing an excuse for their sin.

XXVII. It can no longer be doubtful, therefore, to persons of sound judgment, that the Lord, in that passage, only condemns those oaths which had been forbidden by the law. For even he, who exhibited in his life an example of the perfection which he inculcated, hesitated not to make use of oaths whenever occasion required; and his disciples, who, we doubt not, were obedient to their master in all things, followed the same example. Who can dare to assert, that Paul would have sworn, if all oaths had been prohibited? But when the occasion requires it, he swears without any scruple, and sometimes even adds an imprecation. The question, however, is not yet decided; for it is the opinion of some persons, that public oaths are the only exceptions from this prohibition; such as we take when required by a magistrate; such also as princes are accustomed to use in ratifying treaties; or subjects, when they swear allegiance to their princes; or soldiers, as a military test; and others of a similar kind. To this class also they justly refer those oaths which we find used by Paul in assertion of the dignity of the gospel; because the Apostles, in the exercise of their functions, were not private persons, but public ministers of God. And indeed I will not deny that these are the safest oaths; because they are sanctioned by the strongest testimonies of Scripture. A magistrate is directed, in a dubious case, to put a witness to his oath, and the witness, on the other hand, is required to answer on his oath; and the Apostle says, that human controversies are adjusted by this expedient. In this precept both parties are furnished with a complete justification of their conduct. Moreover we may observe, that among the ancient heathen a public and solemn oath was held in great reverence; but that common ones, which they used in their ordinary intercourse, were not esteemed of any, or of much importance, because they imagined that these were not regarded by the Divine majesty. But it would be too dangerous to condemn private oaths, which are taken, in cases of necessity, with sobriety, integrity, and reverence, since they are supported both by reason and by scriptural examples. For if it be lawful for private persons in an important and serious affair to appeal to God as a judge between them, much more must it be allowable to invoke him as a witness. Your brother will accuse you of perfidy; you endeavour to exculpate yourself; he will not permit himself by any means to be satisfied. If your reputation be endangered by his obstinate malignity, you may, without any offence, appeal to the judgment of God, that in his own time he will manifest your innocence. If the words be strictly examined, it is a less thing to appeal to him as a witness than as a judge. I see not, therefore, why we should assert such an appeal to him to be unlawful. There are not wanting numerous examples of it. If the oath of Abraham and Isaac with Abimelech be alleged to have been taken in a public capacity, certainly Jacob and Laban were private persons, and yet they confirmed the covenant between them by a mutual oath. Boaz was a private person, who confirmed in the same manner his promise of marriage to Ruth. Obadiah was a private person, a righteous man, and one that feared the Lord, who declared with an oath the fact of which he wished to convince Elijah. I can find, therefore, no better rule, than that we regulate our oaths in such a manner, that they be not rash or inconsiderate, wanton or frivolous, but used in cases of real necessity, as for vindicating the glory of the Lord, or promoting the edification of our brother; which is the end of this commandment of the law.

THE FOURTH COMMANDMENT.

Remember the sabbath day, to keep it holy. Six days shalt thou labour, and do all thy work; but the seventh day is the sabbath of the Lord thy God; in it thou shalt not do any work, &c.

XXVIII. The end of this precept is, that, being dead to our own affections and works, we should meditate on the kingdom of God, and be exercised in that meditation in the observance of his institutions. But, as it has an aspect peculiar and distinct from the others, it requires a little different kind of exposition. The fathers frequently call it a shadowy commandment, because it contains the external observance of the day, which was abolished with the rest of the figures at the advent of Christ. And there is much truth in their observation; but it reaches only half of the subject. Wherefore it is necessary to seek further for an exposition, and to consider three causes, on which I think I have observed this commandment to rest. For it was the design of the heavenly Lawgiver, under the rest of the seventh day, to give the people of Israel a figure of the spiritual rest, by which the faithful ought to refrain from their own works, in order to leave God to work within them. His design was, secondly, that there should be a stated day, on which they might assemble together to hear the law and perform the ceremonies, or at least which they might especially devote to meditations on his works; that by this recollection they might be led to the exercises of piety. Thirdly, he thought it right that servants, and persons living under the jurisdiction of others, should be indulged with a day of rest, that they might enjoy some remission from their labour.

XXIX. Yet we are taught in many places that this adumbration of the spiritual rest was the principal design of the sabbath. For the Lord is hardly so strict in his requisitions of obedience to any other precept. When he means to intimate, in the Prophets, that religion is totally subverted, he complains that his sabbaths are polluted, violated, neglected, and profaned; as though, in case of that duty being neglected, there remained no other way in which he could be honoured. On the other hand, he notices the observance of it with singular encomiums. Wherefore also, among the other Divine communications, the faithful used very highly to esteem the revelation of the sabbath. For this is the language of the Levites in a solemn assembly, recorded by Nehemiah: "Thou madest known unto our fathers thy holy sabbath, and commandedst them precepts, statutes, and laws, by the hand of Moses." We see the singular estimation in which it is held above all the commandments of the law. All these things tend to display the dignity of the mystery, which is beautifully expressed by Moses and Ezekiel. In Exodus we read as follows: "Verily my sabbaths ye shall keep; for it is a sign between me and you throughout your generations; that ye may know that I am the Lord that doth sanctify you. Ye shall keep the sabbath therefore; for it is holy unto you. The children of Israel shall keep the sabbath, to observe the sabbath throughout their generations, for a perpetual covenant. It is a sign between me and the children of Israel for ever." This is more fully expressed by Ezekiel; but the substance of what he says is, that the sabbath was a sign by which the Israelites might know that God was their sanctifier. If our sanctification consists properly in the mortification of our own will, there is a very natural analogy between the external sign and the internal thing which it represents.

We must rest altogether, that God may operate within us; we must recede from our own will, resign our own heart, and renounce all our carnal affections; in short, we must cease from all the efforts of our own understanding, that having God operating within us, we may enjoy rest in him, as we are also taught by the Apostle.

XXX. This perpetual cessation was represented to the Jews by the observance of one day in seven, which the Lord, in order that it might be the more religiously kept, recommended by his own example. For it is no small stimulus to any action, for a man to know that he is imitating his Creator. If any one inquire after a hidden signification in the septenary number, it is probable, that because in Scripture it is the number of perfection, it is here selected to denote perpetual duration. This is confirmed also by the circumstance, that Moses, with that day in which he narrates that the Lord rested from his works, concludes his description of the succession of days and nights. We may also adduce another probable conjecture respecting this number—that the Lord intended to signify that the sabbath would never be completed until the arrival of the last day. For in it we begin that blessed rest, in which we make new advances from day to day. But because we are still engaged in a perpetual warfare with the flesh, it will not be consummated before the completion of that prediction of Isaiah, "It shall come to pass, that from one new moon to another, and from one sabbath to another, shall all flesh come to worship before me, saith the Lord;" that is, when God shall be "all in all." The Lord may be considered, therefore, as having delineated to his people, in the seventh day, the future perfection of his sabbath in the last day, that, by a continual meditation on the sabbath during their whole life, they might be aspiring towards this perfection.

XXXI. If any one disapprove of this observation on the number, as too curious, I object not to its being understood in a more simple manner; that the Lord ordained a certain day, that the people under the discipline of the law might be exercised in continual meditations on the spiritual rest; that he appointed the seventh day, either because he foresaw it would be sufficient, or in order that the proposal of a resemblance to his own example might operate as a stronger stimulus to the people, or at least to apprize them that the only end of the sabbath was to promote their conformity to their Creator. For this is of little importance, provided we retain the mystery, which is principally exhibited, of a perpetual rest from our own works. To the contemplation of this, the Prophets used frequently to recall the Jews, that they might not suppose themselves to have discharged their duty merely by a cessation from manual labours. Beside the passages already cited, we have the following in Isaiah: "If thou turn away thy foot from the sabbath, from doing thy pleasure on my holy day; and call the sabbath a delight, the holy of the Lord, honourable; and shalt honour him, not doing thine own ways, nor finding thine own pleasure, nor speaking thine own words; then shalt thou delight thyself in the Lord," &c. But all that it contained of a ceremonial nature was without doubt abolished by the advent of the Lord Christ. For he is the truth, at whose presence all figures disappear; the body, at the sight of which all the shadows are relinquished. He, I say, is the true fulfilment of the sabbath. Having been "buried with him by baptism, we have been planted together in the likeness of his death, that being partakers of his resurrection, we may walk in newness of life." Therefore the Apostle says in another place, that "the sabbath was a shadow of things to come; but the body is of Christ;" that is, the real substance of the truth, which he has beautifully explained in that passage. This is contained not in one day, but in the whole course of our life, till, being wholly dead to ourselves, we be filled with the life of God. Christians therefore ought to depart from all superstitious observance of days.

XXXII. As the two latter causes, however, ought not to be numbered among the ancient shadows, but are equally suitable to all ages,—though the sabbath is abrogated, yet it is still customary among us to assemble on stated days for hearing the word, for breaking the mystic bread, and for public prayers; and also to allow servants and labourers a remission from their labour. That in commanding the sabbath, the Lord had regard to both these things, cannot be doubted. The first is abundantly confirmed even by the practice of the Jews. The second is proved by Moses, in Deuteronomy, in these words: "that thy man-servant and thy maid-servant may rest as well as thou. And remember that thou wast a servant in the land of Egypt." Also, in Exodus: "that thine ox and thine ass may rest, and the son of thy handmaid, and the stranger, may be refreshed." Who can deny that both these things are as proper for us as for the Jews? Assemblies of the Church are enjoined in the Divine word, and the necessity of them is sufficiently known even from the experience of life. Unless there be stated days appointed for them, how can they be held? According to the direction of the Apostle, "all things" are to "be done decently and in order" among us. But so far is it from being possible to preserve order and decorum without this regulation, that, if it were abolished, the Church would be in imminent danger of immediate convulsion and ruin. But if we feel the same necessity, to relieve which the Lord enjoined the sabbath upon the Jews, let no one plead that it does not belong to us. For our most provident and indulgent Father has been no less attentive to provide for our necessity than for that of the Jews. But why, it may be asked, do we not rather assemble on every day, that so all distinction of days may be removed? I sincerely wish that this were practised; and truly spiritual wisdom would be well worthy of some portion of time being daily allotted to it; but if the infirmity of many persons will not admit of daily assemblies, and charity does not permit us to require more of them, why should we not obey the rule which we have imposed upon us by the will of God?

XXXIII. I am obliged to be rather more diffuse on this point, because, in the present age, some unquiet spirits have been raising noisy contentions respecting the Lord's day. They complain that Christians are tinctured with Judaism, because they retain any observance of days. But I reply, that the Lord's day is not observed by us upon the principles of Judaism; because in this respect the difference between us and the Jews is very great. For we celebrate it not with scrupulous rigour, as a ceremony which we conceive to be a figure of some spiritual mystery, but only use it as a remedy necessary to the preservation of order in the Church. But they say, Paul teaches that Christians are not to be judged in the observance of it, because it is a shadow of something future. Therefore he is "afraid lest" he has "bestowed" on the Galatians "labour in vain," because they continued to "observe days." And in the Epistle to the Romans, he asserts him to be "weak in the faith," who "esteemeth one day above another." But who, these furious zealots only excepted, does not see what observance the apostle intends? For they did not observe them for the sake of political and ecclesiastical order; but when they retained them as shadows of spiritual things, they were so far guilty of obscuring the glory of Christ and the light of the gospel. They did not, therefore, rest from their manual labours, as from employments which would divert them from sacred studies and meditations; but from a principle of superstition, imagining their cessation from labour to be still an expression of reverence for the mysteries formerly represented by it. This preposterous distinction of days the Apostle strenuously opposes; and not that legitimate difference which promotes the peace of the Christian Church. For in the churches which he founded, the sabbath was retained for this purpose. He prescribes the same day to the Corinthians, for making collections for the relief of the brethren at Jerusalem. If superstition be an object of fear, there was more danger in the holy days of the Jews, than in the Lord's days now observed by Christians. Now, whereas it was expedient for the destruction of superstition, the day which the Jews kept holy was abolished; and it being necessary for the preservation of decorum, order, and peace, in the Christian Church, another day was appointed for the same use.

XXXIV. However, the ancients have not without sufficient reason substituted what we call the Lord's day in the room of the sabbath. For since the resurrection of the Lord is the end and consummation of that true rest, which was adumbrated by the ancient sabbath, the same day which put an end to the shadows, admonishes Christians not to adhere to a shadowy ceremony. Yet I do not lay so much stress on the septenary number, that I would oblige the Church to an invariable adherence to it; nor will I condemn those churches which have other solemn days for their assemblies, provided they keep at a distance from superstition. And this will be the case, if they be only designed for the observance of discipline and well-regulated order. Let us sum up the whole in the following manner: As the truth was delivered to the Jews under a figure, so it is given to us without any shadows; first, in order that during our whole life we should meditate on a perpetual rest from our own works, that the Lord may operate within us by his Spirit; secondly, that every man, whenever he has leisure, should diligently exercise himself in private in pious reflections on the works of God, and also that we should at the same time observe the legitimate order of the Church, appointed for the hearing of the word, for the administration of the sacraments, and for public prayer; thirdly, that we should not unkindly oppress those who are subject to us. Thus vanish all the dreams of false prophets, who in past ages have infected the people with a Jewish notion, affirming that nothing but the ceremonial part of this commandment, which, according to them, is the appointment of the seventh day, has been abrogated, but that the moral part of it, that is, the observance of one day in seven, still remains. But this is only changing the day in contempt of the Jews, while they retain the same opinion of the holiness of a day; for on this principle the same mysterious signification would still be attributed to particular days, which they formerly obtained among the Jews. And indeed we see what advantages have arisen from such a sentiment. For those who adhere to it, far exceed the Jews in a gross, carnal, and superstitious observance of the sabbath; so that the reproofs, which we find in Isaiah, are equally applicable to them in the present age, as to those whom the Prophet reproved in his time. But the principal thing to be remembered is the general doctrine; that, lest religion decay or languish among us, sacred assemblies ought diligently to be held, and that we ought to use those external means which are adapted to support the worship of God.

THE FIFTH COMMANDMENT.

Honour thy father and thy mother; that thy days may be long upon the land which the Lord thy God giveth thee.

XXXV. The end of this precept is, that since the Lord God desires the preservation of the order he has appointed, the degrees of preëminence fixed by him ought to be inviolably preserved. The sum of it, therefore, will be, that we should reverence them whom God has exalted to any authority over us, and should render them honour, obedience, and gratitude. Whence follows a prohibition to derogate from their dignity by contempt, obstinacy, or ingratitude. For in the Scripture the word "honour" has an extensive signification; as, when the Apostle directs that "the elders who rule well be counted worthy of double honour," he means not only that they are entitled to reverence, but likewise such a remuneration as their ministry deserves. But as this precept, which enjoins subjection to superiors, is exceedingly repugnant to the depravity of human nature, whose ardent desire of exaltation will scarcely admit of subjection, it has therefore proposed as an example that kind of superiority which is naturally most amiable and least invidious; because that might the more easily mollify and incline our minds to a habit of submission. By that subjection, therefore, which is most easy to be borne, the Lord accustoms us by degrees to every kind of legitimate obedience; because the reason of all is the same. For to those, to whom he gives any preëminence, he communicates his own authority, as far as is necessary for the preservation of that preëminence. The titles of Father, God, and Lord, are so eminently applicable to him, that, whenever we hear either of them mentioned, our minds cannot but be strongly affected with a sense of his majesty. Those, therefore, on whom he bestows these titles, he illuminates with a ray of his splendour, to render them all honourable in their respective stations. Thus in a father we ought to recognize something Divine; for it is not without reason that he bears one of the titles of the Deity. Our prince, or our lord, enjoys an honour somewhat similar to that which is given to God.

XXXVI. Wherefore it ought not to be doubted that God here lays down a universal rule for our conduct; namely, that to every one, whom we know to be placed in authority over us by his appointment, we should render reverence, obedience, gratitude, and all the other services in our power. Nor does it make any difference, whether they are worthy of this honour, or not. For whatever be their characters, yet it is not without the appointment of the Divine providence, that they have attained that station, on account of which the supreme Legislator has commanded them to be honoured. He has particularly enjoined reverence to our parents, who have brought us into this life; which nature itself ought to teach us. For those who violate the parental authority by contempt or rebellion, are not men, but monsters. Therefore the Lord commands all those, who are disobedient to their parents, to be put to death, as having rendered themselves unworthy to enjoy the light, by their disregard of those by whose means they were introduced to it. And various appendices to the law evince the truth of our observation, that the honour here intended consists in reverence, obedience, and gratitude. The first the Lord confirms, when he commands him to be slain who has cursed his father or mother; for in that case he punishes contempt. He confirms the second, when he denounces the punishment of death against disobedient and rebellious children. The third is supported by Christ, who says, "God commanded, saying, Honour thy father and mother;" and, "He that curseth father or mother, let him die the death. But ye say, Whosoever shall say to his father or his mother, It is a gift, by whatsoever thou mightest be profited by me; and honour not his father or his mother, he shall be free. Thus have ye made the commandment of God of none effect by your tradition." And whenever Paul mentions this commandment, he explains it as a requisition of obedience.

XXXVII. In order to recommend it, a promise is annexed, which is a further intimation how acceptable to God that submission is which is here enjoined. Paul employs that stimulus to arouse our inattention, when he says, "This is the first commandment with promise." For the preceding promise, in the first table, was not particularly confined to one commandment, but extended to the whole law. Now, the true explanation of this promise is, that the Lord spake particularly to the Israelites concerning the land which he had promised them as an inheritance. If the possession of that land therefore was a pledge of the Divine goodness, we need not wonder, if it was the Lord's will to manifest his favour by bestowing length of life, in order to prolong the enjoyment of the blessing conferred by him. The meaning of it therefore is, Honour thy father and thy mother, that through the space of a long life thou mayest enjoy the possession of the land, which will be to thee a testimony of my favour. But, as the whole earth is blessed to the faithful, we justly place the present life among the blessings we receive from God. Wherefore this promise belongs likewise to us, inasmuch as the continuance of the present life affords us a proof of the Divine benevolence. For neither is it promised to us, nor was it promised to the Jews, as though it contained any blessedness in itself; but because to the pious it is generally a token of the Divine favour. Therefore, if a son, that is obedient to his parents, happen to be removed out of life before the age of maturity,—which is a case of frequent occurrence,—the Lord, nevertheless, perseveres with as much punctuality in the completion of his promise, as if he were to reward a person with a hundred acres of land to whom he had only promised one. The whole consists in this: We should consider that long life is promised to us so far as it is the blessing of God; but that it is a blessing, only as it is a proof of the favour of God, which he infinitely more richly and substantially testifies and actually demonstrates to his servants in their death.

XXXVIII. Moreover, when the Lord promises the blessing of the present life to those children who honour their parents with proper reverence, he at the same time implies that a certain curse impends over all those who are disobedient and perverse. And that it might not fail of being executed, he pronounces them in his law to be liable to the sentence of death, and commands that punishment to be inflicted on them. If they escape that, he punishes them himself in some other way. For we see what great numbers of persons of this character fall in battles and in private quarrels; others are afflicted in unusual ways; and almost all of them are proofs of the truth of this threatening. But if any arrive at an extreme age, being deprived of the Divine blessing, they only languish in misery in this life, and are reserved to greater punishments hereafter; and consequently they are far from participating in the blessing promised to dutiful children. But it must be remarked by the way, that we are commanded to obey them only "in the Lord;" and this is evident from the foundation before laid; for they preside in that station to which the Lord has exalted them by communicating to them a portion of his honour. Wherefore the submission exercised towards them ought to be a step towards honouring the Supreme Father. Therefore, if they instigate us to any transgression of the law, we may justly consider them not as parents, but as strangers, who attempt to seduce us from obedience to our real Father. The same observation is applicable to princes, lords, and superiors of every description. For it is infamous and absurd, that their eminence should avail to depreciate the preëminence of God, upon which it depends, and to which it ought to conduct us.

THE SIXTH COMMANDMENT.

Thou shalt not kill.

XXXIX. The end of this precept is, that since God has connected mankind together in a kind of unity, every man ought to consider himself as charged with the safety of all. In short, then, all violence and injustice, and every kind of mischief, which may injure the body of our neighbour, are forbidden to us. And therefore we are enjoined, if it be in our power, to assist in protecting the lives of our neighbours; to exert ourselves with fidelity for this purpose; to procure those things which conduce to their tranquillity; to be vigilant in shielding them from injuries; and in cases of danger to afford them our assistance. If we remember that this is the language of the Divine Legislator, we should consider, at the same time, that he intends this rule to govern the soul. For it were ridiculous, that he who beholds the thoughts of the heart, and principally insists on them, should content himself with forming only the body to true righteousness. Mental homicide, therefore, is likewise prohibited, and an internal disposition to preserve the life of our brother is commanded in this law. The hand, indeed, accomplishes the homicide, but it is conceived by the mind under the influence of anger and hatred. Examine whether you can be angry with your brother, without being inflamed with a desire of doing him some injury. If you cannot be angry with him, then you cannot hate him; for hatred is nothing more than inveterate anger. However you may dissemble, and endeavour to extricate yourself by vain subterfuges, whenever there is either anger or hatred, there is also a disposition to do injury. If you persist in your evasions, it is already pronounced by the Holy Spirit, that "Whosoever hateth his brother is a murderer." It is declared by the Lord Christ, "that whosoever is angry with his brother without a cause shall be in danger of the judgment; and whosoever shall say to his brother, Raca, shall be in danger of the council; but whosoever shall say, Thou fool, shall be in danger of hell fire."

XL. Now, the Scripture states two reasons on which this precept is founded; the first, that man is the image of God; the second, that he is our own flesh. Wherefore, unless we would violate the image of God, we ought to hold the personal safety of our neighbour inviolably sacred; and unless we would divest ourselves of humanity, we ought to cherish him as our own flesh. The motives which are derived from the redemption and grace of Christ will be treated in another place. These two characters, which are inseparable from the nature of man, God requires us to consider as motives to our exertions for his security; so that we may reverence his image impressed on him, and show an affectionate regard for our own flesh. That person, therefore, is not innocent of the crime of murder, who has merely restrained himself from the effusion of blood. If you perpetrate, if you attempt, if you only conceive in your mind any thing inimical to the safety of another, you stand guilty of murder. Unless you also endeavour to defend him to the utmost of your ability and opportunity, you are guilty of the same inhuman transgression of the law. But if so much concern be discovered for the safety of the body, we may conclude, how much care and attention should be devoted to the safety of the soul, which, in the sight of God, is of infinitely superior value.

THE SEVENTH COMMANDMENT.

Thou shalt not commit adultery.

XLI. The end of this precept is, that because God loves chastity and purity, we ought to depart from all uncleanness. The sum of it therefore is, that we ought not to be polluted by any carnal impurity, or libidinous intemperance. To this prohibition corresponds the affirmative injunction, that every part of our lives ought to be regulated by chastity and continence. But he expressly forbids adultery, to which all incontinence tends; in order that by the turpitude of that which is very gross and palpable, being an infamous pollution of the body, he may lead us to abominate every unlawful passion. Since man was created in such a state as not to live a solitary life, but to be united to a help-meet; and moreover since the curse of sin has increased this necessity,—the Lord has afforded us ample assistance in this case by the institution of marriage—a connection which he has not only originated by his authority, but also sanctified by his blessing. Whence it appears, that every other union, but that of marriage, is cursed in his sight; and that the conjugal union itself is appointed as a remedy for our necessity, that we may not break out into unrestrained licentiousness. Let us not flatter ourselves, therefore, since we hear that there can be no cohabitation of male and female, except in marriage, without the curse of God.

XLII. Now, since the original constitution of human nature, and the violence of the passions consequent upon the fall, have rendered a union of the sexes doubly necessary, except to those whom God has exempted from that necessity by peculiar grace, let every one carefully examine what is given to him. Virginity, I acknowledge, is a virtue not to be despised. But as this is denied to some, and to others is granted only for a season, let those who are troubled with incontinence, and cannot succeed in resisting it, avail themselves of the help of marriage, that they may preserve their chastity according to the degree of their calling. For persons who "cannot receive this saying," if they do not assist their frailty by the remedy offered and granted to them, oppose God and resist his ordinance. Here let no one object, as many do in the present day, that with the help of God he can do all things. For the assistance of God is granted only to them who walk in his ways, that is, in their calling; which is deserted by all those who neglect the means which God has afforded them, and strive to overcome their necessities by vain presumption. That continence is a peculiar gift of God, and of that kind which is not imparted promiscuously, or to the whole body of the Church, but only conferred on a few of its members, is affirmed by our Lord. For he mentions a certain class of men who "have made themselves eunuchs for the kingdom of heaven's sake;" that is, that they might be more at liberty to devote their attention to the affairs of the kingdom of heaven. But that no one might suppose this to be in the power of man, he had already declared that "all men cannot receive this saying, save they to whom it is given." And he concludes, "He that is able to receive it, let him receive it." Paul is still more explicit, when he says, that "every man hath his proper gift of God, one after this manner, and another after that."

XLIII. Since we are so expressly apprized that it is not in the power of every one to preserve chastity in celibacy, even with the most strenuous efforts for that purpose, and that it is a peculiar grace, which the Lord confers only on particular persons, that he may have them more ready for his service, do we not resist God, and strive against the nature instituted by him, unless we accommodate our manner of life to the measure of our ability? In this commandment the Lord prohibits adultery: therefore he requires of us purity and chastity. The only way of preserving this is, that every one should measure himself by his own capacity. Let no one rashly despise marriage as a thing useless or unnecessary to him; let no one prefer celibacy, unless he can dispense with a wife. And in that state let him not consult his carnal tranquillity or advantage, but only that, being exempted from this restraint, he may be the more prompt and ready for all the duties of piety. Moreover, as this benefit is conferred upon many persons only for a season, let every one refrain from marriage as long as he shall be capable of supporting a life of celibacy. When his strength fails to overcome his passions, let him consider that the Lord has laid him under a necessity of marrying. This is evident from the direction of the Apostle: "To avoid fornication, let every man have his own wife, and let every woman have her own husband." Again: "If they cannot contain, let them marry." Here, in the first place, he signifies that the majority of men are subject to the vice of incontinence; in the next place, of those who are subject to it, he makes no exception, but enjoins them all to have recourse to that sole remedy which obviates unchastity. Those who are incontinent, therefore, if they neglect this method of curing their infirmity, are guilty of sin, in not obeying this injunction of the Apostle. And let not him who refrains from actual fornication, flatter himself, as though he could not be charged with unchastity, while his heart at the same time is inflamed with libidinous desire. For Paul defines chastity to consist in sanctity of mind connected with purity of body. "The unmarried woman," he says, "careth for the things of the Lord, that she may be holy both in body and in spirit." Therefore, when he gives a reason to confirm the preceding injunction, he does not content himself with saying that it is better for a man to marry than to pollute himself with the society of a harlot, but affirms that "it is better to marry than to burn."

XLIV. Now, if married persons are satisfied that their society is attended with the blessing of the Lord, they are thereby admonished that it must not be contaminated by libidinous and dissolute intemperance. For if the honour of marriage conceals the shame of incontinence, it ought not on that account to be made an incitement to it. Wherefore let it not be supposed by married persons that all things are lawful to them. Every man should observe sobriety towards his wife, and every wife, reciprocally, towards her husband; conducting themselves in such a manner as to do nothing unbecoming the decorum and temperance of marriage. For thus ought marriage contracted in the Lord to be regulated by moderation and modesty, and not to break out into the vilest lasciviousness. Such sensuality has been stigmatized by Ambrose with a severe, but not unmerited censure, when he calls those who in their conjugal intercourse have no regard to modesty or decorum, the adulterers of their own wives. Lastly, let us consider who the Legislator is, by whom adultery is here condemned. It is no other than he who ought to have the entire possession of us, and justly requires the whole of our spirit, soul, and body. Therefore, when he prohibits us from committing adultery, he at the same time forbids us, either by lasciviously ornamenting our persons, or by obscene gesticulations, or by impure expressions, insidiously to attack the chastity of others. For there is much reason in the address of Archelaus to a young man clothed in an immoderately effeminate and delicate manner, that it was immaterial in what part he was immodest, with respect to God, who abominates all contamination, in whatever part it may discover itself, either of soul or of body. And that there may be no doubt on the subject, let us remember that God here recommends chastity. If the Lord requires chastity of us, he condemns every thing contrary to it. Wherefore, if we aspire to obedience, neither let our mind internally burn with depraved concupiscence, nor let our eyes wanton into corrupt affections, nor let our body be adorned for purposes of seduction, nor let our tongue with impure speeches allure our mind to similar thoughts, nor let us inflame ourselves with intemperance. For all these vices are stains, by which the purity of chastity is defiled.

THE EIGHTH COMMANDMENT.

Thou shalt not steal.

XLV. The end of this precept is, that, as injustice is an abomination to God, every man may possess what belongs to him. The sum of it, then, is, that we are forbidden to covet the property of others, and are therefore enjoined faithfully to use our endeavours to preserve to every man what justly belongs to him. For we ought to consider, that what a man possesses has fallen to his lot, not by a fortuitous contingency, but by the distribution of the supreme Lord of all; and that therefore no man can be deprived of his possessions by criminal methods, without an injury being done to the Divine dispenser of them. But the species of theft are numerous. One consists in violence; when the property of any person is plundered by force and predatory license. Another consists in malicious imposture; when it is taken away in a fraudulent manner. Another consists in more secret cunning; where any one is deprived of his property under the mask of justice. Another consists in flatteries; where we are cheated under the pretence of a donation. But not to dwell too long on the recital of the different species of theft, let us remember that all artifices by which the possessions and wealth of our neighbours are transferred to us, whenever they deviate from sincere love into a desire of deceiving, or doing any kind of injury, are to be esteemed acts of theft. This is the only view in which God considers them, even though the property may be gained by a suit at law. For he sees the tedious manœuvres with which the designing man begins to decoy his more simple neighbour, till at length he entangles him in his snares. He sees the cruel and inhuman laws, by which the more powerful man oppresses and ruins him that is weaker. He sees the baits with which the more crafty trap the imprudent. All which things are concealed from the judgment of man, nor ever come to his knowledge. And this kind of injury relates not only to money, or to goods, or to lands, but to whatever each individual is justly entitled to; for we defraud our neighbours of their property, if we deny them those kind offices, which it is our duty to perform to them. If an idle agent or steward devour the substance of his master, and be inattentive to the care of his domestic affairs; if he either improperly waste, or squander with a luxurious profusion, the property intrusted to him; if a servant deride his master, if he divulge his secrets, if by any means he betray either his life or his property; and if, on the other hand, a master inhumanly oppress his family,—God holds him guilty of theft. For the property of others is withheld and misapplied by him, who does not perform towards them those offices which the duty of his situation requires of him.

XLVI. We shall rightly obey this commandment therefore, if, contented with our own lot, we seek no gain but in an honest and lawful way; if we neither desire to enrich ourselves by injustice, nor attempt to ruin the fortune of our neighbour, in order to increase our own; if we do not labour to accumulate wealth by cruelty, and at the expense of the blood of others; if we do not greedily scrape together from every quarter, regardless of right or wrong, whatever may conduce to satiate our avarice or support our prodigality. On the contrary, it should be our constant aim, as far as possible, faithfully to assist all by our advice and our property in preserving what belongs to them; but if we are concerned with perfidious and fallacious men, let us be prepared rather to recede a little from our just right than to contend with them. Moreover, let us communicate to the necessities, and according to our ability alleviate the poverty, of those whom we perceive to be pressed by any embarrassment of their circumstances. Lastly, let every man examine what obligations his duty lays him under to others, and let him faithfully discharge the duties which he owes them. For this reason the people should honour their governors, patiently submit to their authority, obey their laws and mandates, and resist nothing, to which they can submit consistently with the Divine will. On the other hand, let governors take care of their people, preserve the public peace, protect the good, punish the wicked, and administer all things in such a manner, as becomes those who must render an account of their office to God the supreme Judge. Let the ministers of churches faithfully devote themselves to the ministry of the word, and let them never adulterate the doctrine of salvation, but deliver it pure and uncontaminated to the people of God. Let them teach, not only by their doctrine, but by the example of their lives; in a word, let them preside as good shepherds over the sheep. Let the people, on their part, receive them as the messengers and apostles of God, render to them that honour to which the supreme Master has exalted them, and furnish them with the necessaries of life. Let parents undertake the support, government, and instruction of their children, as committed by God to their care; nor let them exasperate their minds and alienate their affections from them by cruelty, but cherish and embrace them with the lenity and indulgence becoming their character. And that obedience is due to them from their children has been before observed. Let juniors revere old age, since the Lord has designed that age to be honourable. Let old men, by their prudence and superior experience, guide the imbecility of youth; not teasing them with sharp and clamorous invectives, but tempering severity with mildness and affability. Let servants show themselves obedient and diligent in the service of their masters; and that not only in appearance, but from the heart, as serving God himself. Neither let masters behave morosely and perversely to their servants, harassing them with excessive asperity, or treating them with contempt; but rather acknowledge them as their brethren and companions in the service of the heavenly Master, entitled to be regarded with mutual affection, and to receive kind treatment. In this manner, I say, let every man consider what duties he owes to his neighbours, according to the relations he sustains; and those duties let him discharge. Moreover, our attention should always be directed to the Legislator; to remind us that this law is ordained for our hearts as much as for our hands, in order that men may study both to protect the property and to promote the interests of others.

THE NINTH COMMANDMENT.

Thou shalt not bear false witness against thy neighbour.

XLVII. The end of this precept is, that because God, who is truth itself, execrates a lie, we ought to preserve the truth without the least disguise. The sum of it therefore is, that we neither violate the character of any man, either by calumnies or by false accusations, nor distress him in his property by falsehood, nor injure him by detraction or impertinence. This prohibition is connected with an injunction to do all the service we can to every man, by affirming the truth for the protection of his reputation and his property. The Lord seems to have intended the following words as an exposition of this command: "Thou shalt not raise a false report: put not thine hand with the wicked to be an unrighteous witness." Again: "Keep thee far from a false matter." In another place also he not only forbids us to practise backbiting and tale-bearing among the people, but prohibits every man from deceiving his brother; for he cautions us against both in distinct commandments. Indeed there is no doubt but that, as, in the preceding precepts, he has prohibited cruelty, impurity, and avarice, so in this he forbids falsehood; of which there are two branches, as we have before observed. For either we transgress against the reputation of our neighbours by malignity and perverse detraction, or by falsehood and sometimes by obloquy we injure their interests. It is immaterial whether we suppose the testimony here designed to be solemn and judicial, or a common one, which is delivered in private conversations. For we must always recur to this maxim—that, of each of the separate kinds of vices, one species is proposed as an example, to which the rest may be referred; and that, in general, the species selected is that in which the turpitude of the vice is most conspicuous. It is proper, however, to extend it more generally to calumnies and detraction, by which our neighbours are unjustly harassed; because falsehood in a forensic testimony is always attended with perjury. But perjury, being a profanation and violation of the name of God, has already been sufficiently condemned in the third commandment. Wherefore the legitimate observance of this precept is, that our tongue, by asserting the truth, ought to serve both the reputation and the profit of our neighbours. The equity of this is self-evident. For if a good name be more precious than any treasures whatever, a man sustains as great an injury when he is deprived of the integrity of his character, as when he is despoiled of his wealth. And in plundering his substance, there is sometimes as much effected by false testimony, as by the hands of violence.

XLVIII. Nevertheless, it is wonderful with what supine security this precept is generally transgressed, so that few persons can be found, who are not notoriously subject to this malady; we are so fascinated with the malignant pleasure of examining and detecting the faults of others. Nor should we suppose it to be a sufficient excuse, that in many cases we cannot be charged with falsehood. For he who forbids the character of our brother to be bespattered with falsehood, wills also that as far as the truth will permit, it be preserved immaculate. For although he only guards it against falsehood, he thereby suggests that it is committed to his charge. But this should be sufficient to induce us to defend the fair character of our neighbour—that God concerns himself in its protection. Wherefore detraction is, without doubt, universally condemned. Now, by detraction we mean, not reproof, which is given from a motive of correction; not accusation or judicial denunciation, by which recompense is demanded for an injury; not public reprehension, which tends to strike terror into other offenders; not a discovery to them whose safety depends on their being previously warned, that they may not be endangered through ignorance; but odious crimination, which arises from malice, and a violent propensity to detraction. This commandment also extends so far as to forbid us to affect a pleasantry tinctured with scurrilous and bitter sarcasms, severely lashing the faults of others under the appearance of sport; which is the practice of some who aim at the praise of raillery, to the prejudice of the modesty and feelings of others; for such wantonness sometimes fixes a lasting stigma on the characters of our brethren. Now, if we turn our eyes to the Legislator whose proper right it is to rule our ears and our minds, as much as our tongues, it will certainly appear that an avidity of hearing detraction, and an unreasonable propensity to unfavourable opinions respecting others, are equally prohibited. For it would be ridiculous for any one to suppose that God hates slander in the tongue, and does not reprobate malice in the heart. Wherefore, if we possess the true fear and love of God, let us make it our study, that as far as is practicable and expedient, and consistent with charity, we devote neither our tongues nor our ears to opprobrious and malicious raillery, nor inadvertently attend to unfavourable suspicions; but that, putting fair constructions on every man's words and actions, we regulate our hearts, our ears, and our tongues, with a view to preserve the reputation of all around us.

THE TENTH COMMANDMENT.

Thou shalt not covet thy neighbour's house, thou shalt not covet thy neighbour's wife, nor his man-servant, nor his maid-servant, nor his ox, nor his ass, nor any thing that is thy neighbour's.

XLIX. The end of this precept is, that, since it is the will of God that our whole soul should be under the influence of love, every desire inconsistent with charity ought to be expelled from our minds. The sum, then, will be, that no thought should obtrude itself upon us, which would excite in our minds any desire that is noxious, and tends to the detriment of another. To which corresponds the affirmative precept, that all our conceptions, deliberations, resolutions, and undertakings, ought to be consistent with the benefit and advantage of our neighbours. But here we meet with what appears to be a great and perplexing difficulty. For if our previous assertions be true, that the terms adultery and theft comprehend the licentious desire, and the injurious and criminal intention, this may be thought to have superseded the necessity of a separate command being afterwards introduced, forbidding us to covet the possessions of others. But we shall easily solve this difficulty by a distinction between intention and concupiscence. For an intention, as we have before observed in explaining the former commandments, is a deliberate consent of the will, when the mind has been enslaved by any unlawful desire. Concupiscence may exist without such deliberation or consent, when the mind is only attracted and stimulated by vain and corrupt objects. As the Lord, therefore, has hitherto commanded our wills, efforts, and actions to be subject to the law of love, so now he directs that the conceptions of our minds be subject to the same regulation, lest any of them be corrupt and perverted, and give our hearts an improper impulse. As he has forbidden our minds to be inclined and persuaded to anger, hatred, adultery, rapine, and falsehood, so now he prohibits them from being instigated to these vices.

L. Nor is it without cause that he requires such consummate rectitude. For who can deny that it is reasonable for all the powers of our souls to be under the influence of love? But if any one deviate from the path of love, who can deny that that soul is in an unhealthy state? Now, whence is it, that your mind conceives desires prejudicial to your neighbour, but that, neglecting his interest, you consult nothing but your own? For if your heart were full of love, there would be no part of it exposed to such imaginations. It must therefore be destitute of love, so far as it is the seat of concupiscence. Some one will object, that it is unreasonable, that imaginations, which without reflection flutter about in the mind, and then vanish away, should be condemned as symptoms of concupiscence, which has its seat in the heart. I reply, that the present question relates to that kind of imaginations, which, when they are presented to our understandings, at the same time strike our hearts, and inflame them with cupidity; since the mind never entertains a wish for any thing after which the heart is not excited to pant. Therefore God enjoins a wonderful ardour of love, which he will not allow to be interrupted even by the smallest degree of concupiscence. He requires a heart admirably well regulated, which he permits not to be disturbed with the least emotion contrary to the law of love. Do not imagine that this doctrine is unsupported by any great authority; for I derived the first idea of it from Augustine. Now, though the design of the Lord was to prohibit us from all corrupt desires, yet he has exhibited, as examples, those objects which most generally deceive us with a fallacious appearance of pleasure; that he might not leave any thing to concupiscence, after having driven it from those objects towards which it is most violently inclined. Behold, then, the second table of the law, which sufficiently instructs us in the duties we owe to men for the sake of God, on regard to whom the whole rule of love depends. The duties taught in this second table, therefore, we shall inculcate in vain, unless our instruction be founded on the fear and reverence of God. To divide the prohibition of concupiscence into two precepts, the discerning reader, without any comment of mine, will pronounce to be a corrupt and violent separation of what is but one. Nor is the repetition of this phrase, "Thou shalt not covet," any objection against us; because, having mentioned the house or family, God enumerates the different parts of it, beginning with the wife. Hence it clearly appears that it ought to be read, as it is correctly read by the Hebrews, in one continued connection; and in short, that God commands, that all that every man possesses remain safe and entire, not only from any actual injury or fraudulent intention, but even from the least emotion of cupidity that can solicit our hearts.

LI. But what is the tendency of the whole law, will not now be difficult to judge: it is to a perfection of righteousness, that it may form the life of man after the example of the Divine purity. For God has so delineated his own character in it, that the man who exemplifies in his actions the precepts it contains, will exhibit in his life, as it were, an image of God. Wherefore, when Moses would recall the substance of it to the remembrance of the Israelites, he said, "And now, Israel, what doth the Lord thy God require of thee, but to fear the Lord thy God, to walk in all his ways, and to love him, and to serve the Lord thy God with all thy heart, and with all thy soul, to keep the commandments of the Lord?" Nor did he cease to reiterate the same things to them, whenever he intended to point out the end of the law. The tendency of the doctrine of the law is to connect man with his God, and, as Moses elsewhere expresses it, to make him cleave to the Lord in sanctity of life. Now, the perfection of this sanctity consists in two principal points, already recited—"that we love the Lord our God with all our heart, and with all our soul, and with all our strength, and with all our mind; and our neighbour as ourselves." And the first is, that our souls be completely filled with the love of God. From this the love of our neighbour will naturally follow; as the Apostle signifies, when he says, that "the end of the commandment is charity out of a pure heart, and of a good conscience, and of faith unfeigned." Here we find a good conscience and faith unfeigned, that is, in a word, true piety, stated to be the grand source from which charity is derived. He is deceived, therefore, who supposes that the law teaches nothing but certain rudiments and first principles of righteousness, by which men are introduced to the commencement, but are not directed to the true goal of good works; since beyond the former sentence of Moses, and the latter of Paul, nothing further can be wanted to the highest perfection. For how far will he wish to proceed, who will not be content with this instruction, by which man is directed to the fear of God, to the spiritual worship of him, to the observance of his commands, to persevering rectitude in the way of the Lord, to purity of conscience, and sincere faith and love? Hence we derive a confirmation of the foregoing exposition of the law, which traces and finds in its precepts all the duties of piety and love. For they who attend merely to dry and barren elements, as though it taught them but half of the Divine will, are declared by the Apostle to have no knowledge of its end.

LII. But because Christ and his Apostles, in reciting the substance of the law, sometimes omit the first table, many persons are deceived in this point, who wish to extend their expressions to both tables. In the Gospel of Matthew, Christ calls judgment, mercy, and faith, “the weightier matters of the law.” By the word faith it is evident to me that he intends truth or fidelity towards men. Some, however, in order to extend the passage to the whole law, take the word faith to mean religion towards God. But for this there is no foundation; for Christ is treating of those works by which man ought to prove himself to be righteous. If we attend to this observation, we shall cease also to wonder, why, in another place, to the inquiry of a young man, what those commandments are by the observance of which we enter into life, he only returns the following answer: “Thou shalt do no murder, Thou shalt not commit adultery, Thou shalt not steal, Thou shalt not bear false witness, Honour thy father and thy mother; and, Thou shalt love thy neighbour as thyself.” For obedience to the first table consisted chiefly either in the disposition of the heart, or in ceremonies. The disposition of the heart was not visible, and the ceremonies were diligently performed by hypocrites; but the works of charity are such as enable us to give a certain evidence of righteousness. But the same occurs in the Prophets so frequently, that it must be familiar to the reader who is but tolerably conversant with them. For in almost all cases when they exhort to repentance, they omit the first table, and insist on faith, judgment, mercy, and equity. Nor do they by this method neglect the fear of God, but require substantial proof of it from those marks. It is well known that when they treat of the observation of the law, they generally insist on the second table; because it is in it that the love of righteousness and integrity is principally discovered. It is unnecessary to quote the passages, as every person will of himself easily remark what I have stated.

LIII. Is it, then, it will be asked, of more importance towards the attainment of righteousness to live innocently with men, than piously towards God? By no means. But because no man fulfils all the duties of charity, unless he really fear God, we derive from those duties a proof of his piety. Besides, the Lord, well knowing that he can receive no benefit from us, which he also declares by the Psalmist, requires not our services for himself, but employs us in good works towards our neighbour. It is not without reason, then, that the Apostle makes all the perfection of the saints to consist in love; which in another place he very justly styles “the fulfilling of the law;” adding, that “he that loveth another hath fulfilled the law.” Again: that “all the law is fulfilled in one word, even in this, Thou shalt love thy neighbour as thyself.” For he teaches nothing different from what is taught by Christ himself, when he says, “All things whatsoever ye would that men should do to you, do ye even so to them; for this is the law and the prophets.” It is certain that in the law and the prophets, faith, and all that pertains to the legitimate worship of God, hold the principal place, and that love occupies an inferior station; but our Lord intends that the observance of justice and equity among men is only prescribed to us in the law, that our pious fear of him, if we really possess any, may be proved by our actions.

LIV. Here, then, we must rest, that our life will then be governed according to the will of God, and the prescriptions of his law, when it is in all respects most beneficial to our brethren. But we do not find in the whole law one syllable, that lays down any rule for a man respecting those things which he should practise or omit for his carnal convenience. And surely, since men are born in such a state, that they are entirely governed by an immoderate self-love,—a passion which, how great soever their departure from the truth, they always retain,—there was no need of a law which would inflame that love, already of itself too violent. Whence it plainly appears, that the observance of the commandments consists not in the love of ourselves, but in the love of God and of our neighbour; that his is the best and most holy life, who lives as little as possible to himself; and that no man leads a worse or more iniquitous life, than he who lives exclusively to himself, and makes his own interest the sole object of his thoughts and pursuits. Moreover, the Lord, in order to give us the best expression of the strength of that love which we ought to exercise towards our neighbours, has regulated it by the standard of our self-love, because there was no stronger or more vehement affection. And the force of the expression must be carefully examined; for he does not, according to the foolish dreams of some sophists, concede the first place to self-love, and assign the second to the love of our neighbour; but rather transfers to others that affection of love which we naturally restrict to ourselves. Whence the Apostle asserts that "charity seeketh not her own." Nor is their argument, that every thing regulated by any standard is inferior to the standard by which it is regulated, worthy of the least attention. For God does not appoint our self-love as the rule, to which our love to others should be subordinate; but whereas, through our natural depravity, our love used to terminate in ourselves, he shows that it ought now to be diffused abroad; that we may be ready to do any service to our neighbour with as much alacrity, ardour, and solicitude, as to ourselves.

LV. Now, since Christ has demonstrated, in the parable of the Samaritan, that the word "neighbour" comprehends every man, even the greatest stranger, we have no reason to limit the commandment of love to our own relations or friends. I do not deny, that the more closely any person is united to us, the greater claim he has to the assistance of our kind offices. For the condition of humanity requires, that men should perform more acts of kindness to each other, in proportion to the closeness of the bonds by which they are connected, whether of relationship, or acquaintance, or vicinity; and this without any offence to God, by whose providence we are constrained to it. But I assert, that the whole human race, without any exception, should be comprehended in the same affection of love, and that in this respect there is no difference between the barbarian and the Grecian, the worthy and unworthy, the friend and the foe; for they are to be considered in God, and not in themselves, and whenever we deviate from this view of the subject, it is no wonder if we fall into many errors. Wherefore, if we wish to adhere to the true law of love, our eyes must chiefly be directed, not to man, the prospect of whom would impress us with hatred more frequently than with love, but to God, who commands that our love to him be diffused among all mankind; so that this must always be a fundamental maxim with us, that whatever be the character of a man, yet we ought to love him because we love God.

LVI. Wherefore the schoolmen have discovered either their ignorance or their wickedness in a most pestilent manner, when, treating of the precepts prohibiting the desire of revenge, and enjoining the love of our enemies, which were anciently delivered to all the Jews, and afterwards equally to all Christians, they have made them to be counsels which we are at liberty to obey or not to obey, and have confined the necessary observance of them to the monks, who, on account of this very circumstance, would be more righteous than plain Christians, because they voluntarily bound themselves to observe these counsels. The reason which they assign for not receiving them as laws, is, that they appear too burdensome and grievous, especially to Christians who are under the law of grace. Do they presume in this manner to disannul the eternal law of God respecting the love of our neighbour? Is such a distinction to be found in any page of the law? On the contrary, does it not abound with commandments most strictly enjoining the love of our enemies? For what is the meaning of the injunction to feed our neighbour when he is hungry? to direct into the right way his oxen or his asses when they are going astray, and to help them when sinking under a burden? Shall we do good to his cattle for his sake, and feel no benevolence to his person? What! is not the word of the Lord eternal? "Vengeance is mine, I will repay:" which is expressed in another passage still more explicitly: "Thou shalt not avenge, nor bear any grudge against the children of thy people." Let them either obliterate these passages from the law, or acknowledge that the Lord was a Legislator, and no longer falsely pretend that he was only a counsellor.

LVII. And what is the meaning of the following expressions, which they have presumed to abuse by the absurdity of their comment? "Love your enemies, bless them that curse you, do good to them that hate you, and pray for them which despitefully use you, and persecute you; that ye may be the children of your Father which is in heaven." Here, who would not argue with Chrysostom, that the allegation of such a necessary cause clearly proves these to be, not exhortations, but commandments? What have we left us, after being expunged from the number of the children of God? But according to them, the monks will be the only sons of the heavenly Father; they alone will venture to invoke God as their Father. What will now become of the Church? Upon the same principle it will be confined to heathen and publicans. For Christ says, "If ye love them which love you, what reward have ye? do not even the publicans the same?" Shall not we be in a happy situation, if they leave us the title of Christians, but deprive us of the inheritance of the kingdom of heaven? The argument of Augustine is equally strong. When the Lord, says he, prohibits adultery, he forbids you to violate the wife of your enemy no less than of your friend: when he prohibits theft, he permits you not to steal from any one, whether he be a friend or an enemy. Now, Paul reduces these two prohibitions of theft and adultery to the rule of love, and even teaches that they are "briefly comprehended in this saying, namely, Thou shalt love thy neighbour as thyself." Either, then, Paul must have been an erroneous expositor of the law, or it necessarily follows from this, that we are commanded to love, not only our friends, but also our enemies. Those, therefore, who so licentiously shake off the yoke common to the children of God, evidently betray themselves to be the sons of Satan. It is doubtful whether they have discovered greater stupidity or impudence in the publication of this dogma. For all the fathers decidedly pronounce that these are mere precepts. That no doubt was entertained on the subject in the time of Gregory, appears from his positive assertions; for he treats them as precepts, as though it had never been controverted. And how foolishly do they argue! They would be a burden, say they, too grievous for Christians; as though truly any thing could be conceived more difficult, than to love God with all our heart, with all our soul, and with all our strength. Compared with this law, every thing must be accounted easy, whether it be to love an enemy, or to banish from the mind all desire of revenge. To our imbecility, indeed, every thing is arduous and difficult, even the smallest point in the law. It is the Lord in whom we find strength: let him give what he commands, and let him command what he pleases. The being Christians under the law of grace consists not in unbounded license uncontrolled by any law, but in being ingrafted into Christ, by whose grace they are delivered from the curse of the law, and by whose Spirit they have the law inscribed on their hearts. This grace Paul has figuratively denominated a law, in allusion to the law of God, to which he was comparing and contrasting it. Their dispute concerning the word law is a dispute about nothing.

LVIII. Of the same nature is what they have called venial sin—a term which they apply to secret impiety, which is a breach of the first table, and to the direct transgression of the last commandment. For this is their definition, that "it is evil desire without any deliberate assent, and without any long continuance in the heart." Now, I assert that evil desire cannot enter the heart, except through a deficiency of those things which the law requires. We are forbidden to have any strange gods. When the mind, assaulted by mistrust, looks around to some other quarter; when it is stimulated by a sudden desire of transferring its happiness from God to some other being; whence proceed these emotions, however transient, but from the existence of some vacant space in the soul to receive such temptations? And not to protract this argument to greater length, we are commanded to love God with all our heart, with all our mind, and with all our soul: therefore, unless all the powers of our soul be intensely engaged in the love of God, we have already departed from the obedience required by the law; for that the dominion of God is not well established in our conscience, is evident, from the enemies that there rebel against his government, and interrupt the execution of his commands. That the last commandment properly belongs to this point, has been already demonstrated. Have we felt any evil desire in our heart? we are already guilty of concupiscence, and are become at once transgressors of the law; because the Lord forbids us, not only to plan and attempt any thing that would prove detrimental to another, but even to be stimulated and agitated with concupiscence. Now, the curse of God always rests on the transgression of the law. We have no reason, therefore, to exempt even the most trivial emotions of concupiscence from the sentence of death. "In determining the nature of different sins," says Augustine, "let us not use deceitful balances, to weigh what we please and how we please, according to our own humour, saying, This is heavy,—This is light; but let us borrow the Divine balance from the Holy Scriptures, as from the treasury of the Lord, and therein weigh what is heavy; or rather let us weigh nothing ourselves, but acknowledge the weights already determined by the Lord." And what says the Scripture? The assertion of Paul, that "the wages of sin is death," sufficiently demonstrates this groundless distinction to have been unknown to him. As we have already too strong a propensity to hypocrisy, this opiate ought by no means to have been added, to lull our consciences into greater insensibility.

LIX. I wish these persons would consider the meaning of this declaration of Christ: "Whosoever shall break one of these least commandments, and shall teach men so, he shall be called the least in the kingdom of heaven." Are not they of this number, who thus presume to extenuate the transgression of the law, as though it were not worthy of death? But they ought to consider, not merely what is commanded, but who it is that gives the commands; because the smallest transgression of the law, which he has given, is a derogation from his authority. Is the violation of the Divine majesty in any case a trivial thing in their estimation? Lastly, if God has declared his will in the law, whatever is contrary to the law displeases him. Will they pretend that the wrath of

God is so debilitated and disarmed, that the punishment of death cannot immediately follow? He has unequivocally declared, if they could induce themselves to listen to his voice, rather than obscure the plain truth with their frivolous subtleties, "The soul that sinneth, it shall die;" and, which I have before cited, "The wages of sin is death." They acknowledge it to be sin, because it is impossible to deny it; yet they contend that it is not mortal sin. But, as they have hitherto too much resigned themselves to infatuation, they should at length learn to return to the exercise of their reason. If they persevere in their dreams, we will take our leave of them. Let the children of God know that all sin is mortal; because it is a rebellion against the will of God, which necessarily provokes his wrath; because it is a transgression of the law, against which the Divine judgment is universally denounced; and that the offences of the saints are venial, not of their own nature, but because they obtain pardon through the mercy of God.

3. CHRIST, THOUGH KNOWN TO THE JEWS UNDER THE LAW, YET CLEARLY REVEALED ONLY IN THE GOSPEL.

As it was not without reason, or without effect, that God was pleased, in ancient times, to manifest himself as a Father by means of expiations and sacrifices, and that he consecrated to himself a chosen people, there is no doubt that he was known, even then, in the same image in which he now appears to us with meridian splendour. Therefore Malachi, after having enjoined the Jews to attend to the law of Moses, and to persevere in the observance of it, (because after his death there was to be an interruption of the prophetical office,) immediately announces, that "the Sun of righteousness shall arise." In this language he suggests, that the law tended to excite in the pious an expectation of the Messiah that was to come, and that at his advent there was reason to hope for a much greater degree of light. For this reason Peter says that "the Prophets have inquired and searched diligently concerning the salvation," which is now manifested in the gospel; and that "it was revealed to them, that not unto themselves, but unto us, they did minister the things which are now reported unto you by them that have preached the gospel unto you." Not that their instructions were useless to the ancient people, or unprofitable to themselves, but because they did not enjoy the treasure, which God through their hands has transmitted to us. For in the present day, the grace, which was the subject of their testimony, is familiarly exhibited before our eyes; and whereas they had but a small taste, we have offered to us a more copious fruition of it. Therefore Christ, who asserts that "Moses wrote of him," nevertheless extols that measure of grace in which we excel the Jews. Addressing his disciples, he says, "Blessed are your eyes, for they see; and your ears, for they hear." "For I tell you, that many prophets and kings have desired to see those things which ye see, and have not seen them; and to hear those things which ye hear, and have not heard them." This is no small recommendation of the evangelical revelation, that God has preferred us to those holy fathers who were eminent for singular piety. To this declaration that other passage is not at all repugnant, where Christ says, "Abraham saw my day, and was glad." For though his prospect of a thing so very remote was attended with much obscurity, yet there was nothing wanting to the certainty of a well founded hope; and hence that joy which accompanied the holy patriarch even to his death. Neither does this assertion of John the Baptist, "No man hath seen God at any time; the only begotten Son, which is in the bosom of the Father, he hath declared him," exclude the pious, who had died before his time, from a participation of the understanding and light which shine in the person of Christ; but, comparing their condition with ours, it teaches us that we have a clear manifestation of those mysteries, of which they had only an obscure prospect through the medium of shadows; as the author of the Epistle to the Hebrews more copiously and excellently shows, that "God, who at sundry times, and in divers manners, spake in time past unto the fathers by the prophets, hath in these last days spoken unto us by his Son." Therefore, though the only begotten Son, who is now to us "the brightness of the glory, and the express image of the person," of God the Father, was formerly known to the Jews, as we have elsewhere shown by a quotation from Paul, that he was the leader of their ancient deliverance from Egypt; yet this also is a truth, which is asserted by the same Paul in another place, that "God, who commanded the light to shine out of darkness, hath shined in our hearts, to give the light of the knowledge of the glory of God in the face of Jesus Christ." For when he appeared in this his image, he made himself visible, as it were, in comparison with the obscure and shadowy representation of him which had been given before. This renders the ingratitude and obstinacy of those, who shut their eyes amid this meridian blaze, so much the more vile and detestable. And therefore Paul says that Satan, "the god of this world, hath blinded their minds, lest the light of the glorious gospel of Christ should shine unto them."

II. Now, I understand the gospel to be a clear manifestation of the mystery of Christ. I grant indeed, since Paul styles the gospel the doctrine of faith, that whatever promises we find in the law concerning the gracious remission of sins, by which God reconciles men to himself, are accounted parts of it. For he opposes faith to those terrors which torment and harass the conscience, if salvation is to be sought by works. Whence it follows, that taking the word gospel in a large sense, it comprehends all those testimonies, which God formerly gave to the fathers, of his mercy and paternal favour; but it is more eminently applicable to the promulgation of the grace exhibited in Christ. This acceptation is not only sanctioned by common use, but supported by the authority of Christ and the Apostles. Whence it is properly said of him, that he "preached the gospel of the kingdom." And Mark introduces himself with this preface: "The beginning of the gospel of Jesus Christ." But it is needless to collect more passages to prove a thing sufficiently known. Christ, then, by his advent, "hath brought life and immortality to light through the gospel." By these expressions Paul means, not that the fathers were immerged in the shades of death, till the Son of God became incarnate; but, claiming for the gospel this honourable prerogative, he teaches that it is a new and unusual kind of legation, in which God has performed those things that he had promised, that the truth of the promises might appear in the person of his Son. For though the faithful have always experienced the truth of the assertion of Paul, that "all the promises of God in him are Yea, and in him Amen," because they have been sealed in their hearts, yet, since he has completed in his body all the parts of our salvation, the lively exhibition of those things has justly obtained new and singular praise. Hence this declaration of Christ: "Hereafter ye shall see heaven open, and the angels of God ascending and descending upon the Son of man." For though he seems to allude to the ladder which the patriarch Jacob saw in a vision, yet he displays the superior excellence of his advent by this character—that he has opened the gate of heaven to give us free admittance into it.

III. Nevertheless, we must beware of the diabolical imagination of Servetus, who, while he designs to extol the magnitude of the grace of Christ, or at least professes such a design, totally abolishes all the promises, as though they were terminated together with the law. He pretends, that by faith in the gospel we receive the completion of all the promises; as though there were no distinction between us and Christ. I have just observed, that Christ left nothing incomplete of all that was essential to our salvation; but it is not a fair inference, that we already enjoy the benefits procured by him; for this would contradict the declaration of Paul, that "hope is laid up for us." I grant, indeed, that when we believe in Christ, we at the same time pass from death to life; but we should also remember the observation of John, that though "we are now the sons of God, it doth not yet appear what we shall be; but we know that, when he shall appear, we shall be like him; for we shall see him as he is." Though Christ, therefore, offers us in the gospel a present plenitude of spiritual blessings, yet the fruition of them is concealed under the custody of hope, till we are divested of our corruptible body, and transfigured into the glory of him who has gone before us. In the mean time, the Holy Spirit commands us to rely on the promises; and his authority we ought to consider sufficient to silence all the clamours of Servetus. For according to the testimony of Paul, "godliness hath promise of the life that now is, and of that which is to come;" and therefore he boasts of being an Apostle of Christ; "according to the promise of life which is in Christ Jesus." In another place he apprizes us that we have the same promises which were given to the saints in former times. Finally, he represents it as the summit of felicity, that we are sealed with the Holy Spirit of promise. Nor, indeed, have we otherwise any enjoyment of Christ, any further than as we embrace him invested with his promises. Hence it is, that he dwells in our hearts, and yet we live like pilgrims at a distance from him; because "we walk by faith, and not by sight." Nor is there any contrariety in these two positions, that we possess in Christ all that belongs to the perfection of the life of heaven, and yet that faith is a vision of invisible blessings. Only there is a difference to be observed in the nature or quality of the promises; because the gospel affords a clear discovery of that which the law has represented in shadows and types.

IV. This likewise evinces the error of those who never make any other comparison between the Law and the Gospel, than between the merit of works and the gratuitous imputation of righteousness. This antithesis, I grant, is by no means to be rejected; because Paul by the word law frequently intends the rule of a righteous life, in which God requires of us what we owe to him, affording us no hope of life, unless we fulfil every part of it, and, on the contrary, annexing a curse if we are guilty of the smallest transgression. This is the sense in which he uses it in those passages, where he argues that we are accepted by God through grace, and are accounted righteous through his pardon of our sins, because the observance of the law, to which the reward is promised, is not to be found in any man. Paul, therefore, justly represents the righteousness of the law and that of the gospel as opposed to each other. But the gospel has not succeeded the whole law, so as to introduce a different way of salvation; but rather to confirm and ratify the promises of the law, and to connect the body with the shadows. For when Christ says that "the law and the prophets were until John," he does not abandon the fathers to the curse which the slaves of the law cannot escape; he rather implies that they were only initiated in the rudiments of religion, so that they remained far below the sublimity of the evangelical doctrine. Wherefore, when Paul calls the gospel "the power of God unto salvation to every one that believeth," he afterwards adds that it is "witnessed by the law and the prophets." But at the end of the same Epistle, although he asserts that the preaching of Jesus Christ is "the revelation of the mystery which was kept secret since the world began," he qualifies this sentiment with the following explication—that it "is now made manifest, and by the Scriptures of the prophets made known to all nations." Hence we conclude, that when mention is made of the whole law, the gospel differs from it only with respect to a clear manifestation; but on account of the inestimable plenitude of grace, which has been displayed to us in Christ, the celestial kingdom of God is justly said to have been erected in the earth at his advent.

V. Now, John was placed between the Law and the Gospel, holding an intermediate office connected with both. For though, in calling Christ "the Lamb of God" and "the victim for the expiation of sins," he preached the substance of the gospel; yet, because he did not clearly express that incomparable power and glory which afterwards appeared in his resurrection, Christ affirms that he is not equal to the Apostles. This is his meaning in the following words: "Among them that are born of women, there hath not risen a greater than John the Baptist: notwithstanding, he that is least in the kingdom of heaven is greater than he." For he is not there commending the persons of men, but after having preferred John to all the prophets, he allots the highest degree of honour to the preaching of the gospel, which we have elsewhere seen is signified by "the kingdom of heaven." When John himself said that he was only a "voice," as though he were inferior to the prophets, this declaration proceeded not from a pretended humility; he meant to signify that he was not intrusted with a proper embassy, but acted merely in the capacity of a herald, according to the prediction of Malachi: "Behold, I will send you Elijah the prophet before the coming of the great and dreadful day of the Lord." Nor indeed, through the whole course of his ministry, did he aim at any thing but procuring disciples for Christ, which he also proves from Isaiah to have been the commission given him by God. In this sense he was called by Christ "a burning and a shining light," because the full day had not yet arrived. Yet this is no reason why he should not be numbered among the preachers of the gospel, as he used the same baptism which was afterwards delivered to the apostles. But it was not till after Christ was received into the celestial glory, that the more free and rapid progress of the apostles completed what John had begun.

4. THE SIMILARITY OF THE OLD AND NEW TESTAMENTS.

From the preceding observations it may now be evident, that all those persons, from the beginning of the world, whom God has adopted into the society of his people, have been federally connected with him by the same law and the same doctrine which are in force among us: but because it is of no small importance that this point be established, I shall show, by way of appendix, since the fathers were partakers with us of the same inheritance, and hoped for the same salvation through the grace of our common Mediator, how far their condition in this connection was different from ours. For though the testimonies we have collected from the law and the prophets in proof of this, render it sufficiently evident that the people of God have never had any other rule of religion and piety, yet because some writers have raised many disputes concerning the difference of the Old and New Testaments, which may occasion doubts in the mind of an undiscerning reader, we shall assign a particular chapter for the better and more accurate discussion of this subject. Moreover, what would otherwise have been very useful, has now been rendered necessary for us by Servetus and some madmen of the sect of the Anabaptists, who entertain no other ideas of the Israelitish nation, than of a herd of swine, whom they pretend to have been pampered by the Lord in this world, without the least hope of a future immortality in heaven. To defend the pious mind, therefore, from this pestilent error, and at the same time to remove all difficulties which may arise from the mention of a diversity between the Old and New Testaments, let us, as we proceed, examine what similarity there is between them, and what difference; what covenant the Lord made with the Israelites, in ancient times, before the advent of Christ, and what he has entered into with us since his manifestation in the flesh.

II. And, indeed, both these topics may be despatched in one word. The covenant of all the fathers is so far from differing substantially from ours, that it is the very same; it only varies in the administration. But as such extreme brevity would not convey to any man a clear understanding of the subject, it is necessary, if we would do any good, to proceed to a more diffuse explication of it. But in showing their similarity, or rather unity, it will be needless to recapitulate all the particulars which have already been mentioned, and unseasonable to introduce those things which remain to be discussed in some other place. We must here insist chiefly on three principal points. We have to maintain, First, that carnal opulence and felicity were not proposed to the Jews as the mark towards which they should ultimately aspire, but that they were adopted to the hope of immortality, and that the truth of this adoption was certified to them by oracles, by the law, and by the prophets. Secondly, that the covenant, by which they were united to the Lord, was founded, not on any merits of theirs, but on the mere mercy of God who called them. Thirdly, that they both possessed and knew Christ as the Mediator, by whom they were united to God, and became partakers of his promises. The second of these points, as perhaps it is not yet sufficiently known, shall be demonstrated at large in its proper place. For we shall prove by numerous and explicit testimonies of the prophets, that whatever blessing the Lord ever gave or promised to his people, proceeded from his indulgent goodness. The third point has been clearly demonstrated in several places. And we have not wholly neglected the first.

III. In discussing the first point, therefore, because it principally belongs to the present argument, and is the grand subject of their controversy against us, we will use the more diligent application; yet in such a manner, that if any thing be wanting to the explication of the others, it may be supplied as we proceed, or added afterwards in a suitable place. Indeed, the apostle removes every doubt respecting all these points, when he says, that God the Father "promised afore by his prophets in the holy Scriptures, the gospel concerning his Son," which he promulgated in the appointed time: and again, that the righteousness of faith, which is revealed in the gospel, is "witnessed by the law and the prophets." For the gospel does not detain men in the joy of the present life, but elevates them to the hope of immortality; does not fasten them to terrestrial delights, but announcing to them a hope reserved in heaven, does as it were transport them thither. For this is the description which he gives in another place: "In whom also after that ye believed, ye were sealed with that Holy Spirit of promise, which is the earnest of our inheritance until the redemption of the purchased possession." Again: "We heard of your faith in Christ Jesus, and of the love which ye have to all the saints, for the hope which is laid up for you in heaven, whereof ye heard before in the word of the truth of the gospel." Again: "He called you by our gospel, to the obtaining of the glory of our Lord Jesus Christ." Whence it is called "the word of salvation," and "the power of God to the salvation of believers," and "the kingdom of heaven." Now, if the doctrine of the gospel be spiritual, and open a way to the possession of an immortal life, let us not suppose that they, to whom it was promised and announced, were totally negligent and careless of their souls, and stupefied in the pursuit of corporeal pleasures. Nor let any one here cavil, that the promises which are recorded in the law and the prophets, respecting the gospel, were not designed for the Jews. For just after having spoken of the gospel being promised in the law, he adds, "that what things soever the law saith, it saith to them who are under the law." This was in another argument, I grant; but when he said that whatever the law inculcates truly belonged to the Jews, he was not so forgetful as not to remember what he had affirmed, a few verses before, concerning the gospel promised in the law. By declaring that the Old Testament contained evangelical promises, therefore, the apostle most clearly demonstrates that it principally related to a future life.

IV. For the same reason it follows, that it was founded on the free mercy of God, and confirmed by the mediation of Christ. For even the preaching of the gospel only announces, that sinners are justified by the paternal goodness of God, independently of any merit of their own; and the whole substance of it terminates in Christ. Who, then, dares to represent the Jews as destitute of Christ,—them with whom we are informed the evangelical covenant was made, of which Christ is the sole foundation? Who dares to represent them as strangers to the benefit of a free salvation, to whom we are informed the doctrine of the righteousness of faith was communicated? But not to be prolix in disputing on a clear point, we have a remarkable expression of the Lord: "Abraham rejoiced to see my day; and he saw it, and was glad." And what Christ there declares concerning Abraham, the apostle shows to have been universal among the faithful, when he says that Christ remains "the same yesterday, and to-day, and for ever." For he there speaks, not only of the eternal Divinity of Christ, but of his power, which has been perpetually manifested to the faithful. Wherefore both the blessed Virgin and Zachariah declare, in their songs, that the salvation revealed in Christ is a performance of the promises which the Lord had made to Abraham and the patriarchs. If the Lord, in the manifestation of Christ, faithfully performed his ancient oath, it cannot be denied that the end of the Old Testament was always in Christ and eternal life.

V. Moreover the apostle makes the Israelites equal to us, not only in the grace of the covenant, but also in the signification of the sacraments. For when he means to adduce examples of the punishments with which the Scripture states them to have been formerly chastised, in order to deter the Corinthians from running into similar crimes, he begins by premising, that we have no reason to arrogate any preëminence to ourselves, which can deliver us from the Divine vengeance inflicted on them; since the Lord not only favoured them with the same benefits, but illustrated his grace among them by the same symbols; as though he had said, If ye confide in being beyond the reach of danger, because both baptism by which you have been sealed, and the supper which you daily receive, have excellent promises, while at the same time you despise the Divine goodness, and live licentious lives,—know ye, that the Jews also were not destitute of such symbols, though the Lord inflicted on them his severest judgments. They were baptized in their passage through the sea, and in the cloud by which they were protected from the fervour of the sun. Our opponents maintain that passage to have been a carnal baptism, corresponding in some degree to our spiritual one. But if that were admitted, the apostle's argument would not proceed; for his design here is to prevent Christians from supposing that they excel the Jews in the privilege of baptism. Nor is what immediately follows, that they "did all eat the same spiritual meat, and did all drink the same spiritual drink," which he interprets of Christ, liable to this cavil.

VI. To invalidate this declaration of Paul, they object the assertion of Christ, "Your fathers did eat manna in the wilderness, and are dead. If any man eat of this bread, (that is, my flesh,) he shall live for ever." But the two passages are reconciled without any difficulty. The Lord, because he was addressing auditors who only sought to be satisfied with corporeal sustenance, but were unconcerned about food for the soul, accommodates his discourse in some measure to their capacity, and institutes a comparison between manna and his own body, particularly to strike their senses. They demand that in order to acquire authority to himself, he should prove his power by some miracle, such as Moses performed in the desert, when he obtained manna from heaven. In the manna, however, they had no idea of any thing but a remedy for corporeal hunger, with which the people were then afflicted. They did not penetrate to that sublimer mystery of which Paul treats. Christ, therefore, to demonstrate the superiority of the blessing they ought to expect from him, to that which they said their fathers had received from Moses, makes this comparison: If it be in your opinion a great and memorable miracle, that the Lord, to prevent his people from perishing in the wilderness, supplied them, by means of Moses, with heavenly food, which served them as a temporary sustenance,—hence conclude how much more excellent that food must be, which communicates immortality. We see, then, why the Lord omitted the principal thing designed by the manna, and only remarked the lowest advantage that resulted from it. It was because the Jews, as if with an intention of reproaching him, contrasted him with Moses, who had supplied the necessities of the people with manna. He replies, that he is the dispenser of a far superior favour, in comparison with which the corporeal sustenance of the people, the sole object of their great admiration, deserves to be considered as nothing. Knowing that the Lord, when he rained manna from heaven, not only poured it down for the support of their bodies, but likewise dispersed it as a spiritual mystery, to typify that spiritual vivification which is experienced in Christ, Paul does not neglect that view of the subject which is most deserving of consideration. Wherefore it is certainly and clearly proved, that the same promises of an eternal and heavenly life, with which the Lord now favours us, were not only communicated to the Jews, but even sealed and confirmed by sacraments truly spiritual. This subject is argued at length by Augustine against Faustus the Manichæan.

VII. But if the reader would prefer a recital of testimonies from the law and the prophets, to show him that the spiritual covenant was common also to the fathers, as we have heard from Christ and his apostles,—I will attend to this wish, and that with the greater readiness, because our adversaries will thereby be more decisively confuted, and will have no pretence for any future cavil. I will begin with that demonstration, which, though I know the Anabaptists will superciliously deem it futile and almost ridiculous, yet will have considerable weight with persons of docility and good understanding. And I take it for granted, that there is such a vital efficacy in the Divine word as to quicken the souls of all those whom God favours with a participation of it. For the assertion of Peter has ever been true, that it is "an incorruptible seed, which abideth for ever;" as he also concludes from the words of Isaiah. Now, when God anciently united the Jews with himself in this sacred bond, there is no doubt that he separated them to the hope of eternal life. For when I say, that they embraced the word which was to connect them more closely with God, I advert not to that general species of communication with him, which is diffused through heaven and earth, and all the creatures in the universe, which although it animates all things according to their respective natures, yet does not deliver from the necessity of corruption. I refer to that particular species of communication, by which the minds of the pious are enlightened into the knowledge of God, and in some measure united to him. Since Adam, Abel, Noah, Abraham, and the other patriarchs, were attached to God by such an illumination of his word, I maintain, there can be no doubt that they had an entrance into his immortal kingdom. For it was a real participation of God, which cannot be separated from the blessing of eternal life.

VIII. If the subject still appear involved in any obscurity, let us proceed to the very form of the covenant; which will not only satisfy sober minds, but will abundantly prove the ignorance of those who endeavour to oppose it. For the Lord has always made this covenant with his servants: "I will be your God, and ye shall be my people." These expressions, according to the common explanation of the prophets, comprehend life, and salvation, and consummate felicity. For it is not without reason that David frequently pronounces, how "blessed is the nation whose God is the Lord; and the people whom he hath chosen for his own inheritance;" and that not on account of any earthly felicity, but because he delivers from death, perpetually preserves, and attends with everlasting mercy, those whom he has taken for his people. As it is expressed in the other prophets, "Art thou not from everlasting, O Lord my God, mine Holy One? we shall not die." "The Lord is our Lawgiver, the Lord is our King; he will save us." "Happy art thou, O Israel: who is like unto thee, O people saved by the Lord?" But not to labour much on a point which does not require it, we are frequently reminded, in reading the prophets, that we shall have a plenitude of all blessings, and even a certainty of salvation, provided the Lord be our God. And that on good ground; for if his face, as soon as it has begun to shine, be a present pledge of salvation, will God manifest himself to any man without opening the treasures of salvation to him? For God is our God, on the express condition of his "walking in the midst of us," as he declared by Moses. But this presence of his cannot be obtained without the possession of life. And though nothing further had been expressed, they had a promise of spiritual life sufficiently clear in these words: "I am the Lord your God." For he announced that he would be a God, not only to their bodies, but chiefly to their souls; for the soul, unless united to God by righteousness, remains alienated from him at death. But let that union take place, and it will be attended with eternal salvation.

IX. Moreover, he not only declared himself to be their God, but promised to continue so for ever; in order that their hope, not contented with present blessings, might be extended to eternity. And that the use of the future tense conveyed this idea to them, appears from many expressions, where the faithful console themselves not only amidst present evils, but for futurity, that God will never desert them. But in regard to the second part of the promise, he still more plainly encouraged them concerning the extension of the Divine blessing to them beyond the limits of the present life: "I will be a God to thy seed after thee." For if he intended to declare his benevolence to them after they were dead, by blessing their posterity, much more would he not fail of manifesting his favour towards themselves. For God is not like men, who transfer their love to the children of their friends, because death takes away their opportunity of performing kind offices to those who were objects of their regard. But God, whose beneficence is not interrupted by death, deprives not the dead of the blessings of his mercy, which for their sakes he diffuses through a thousand generations. The design of the Lord, therefore, was to show them, by a clear proof, the magnitude and abundance of his goodness which they should experience after death, when he described its exuberance as reaching to all their posterity. Now, the Lord sealed the truth, and, as it were, exhibited the completion of this promise, when he called himself the God of Abraham, Isaac, and Jacob, long after they were dead. For what is implied in it? Would it not have been a ridiculous appellation, if they had perished? It would have been just as if he had said, I am the God of those who have no existence. Wherefore, the evangelists relate, that with this single argument the Sadducees were so embarrassed by Christ, as to be unable to deny that Moses had given a testimony in favour of the resurrection of the dead; for they had learned from Moses himself, that "all his saints are in his hand." Whence it was easy to infer, that death had not annihilated those whom he, who is the arbiter of life and death, had received into his guardianship and protection.

X. Now, to come to the principal point on which this controversy turns, let us examine, whether the faithful themselves were not so instructed by the Lord, as to be sensible that they had a better life in another world, and to meditate on that to the neglect of the present. In the first place, the course of life which was divinely enjoined them was a perpetual exercise, by which they were reminded that they were the most miserable of all mankind, if they had no happiness but in the present life. Adam, rendered most unhappy by the mere remembrance of his lost felicity, finds great difficulty in supplying his wants by anxious toils. Nor does the Divine malediction confine itself to his manual labours; he experiences the bitterest sorrow from that which was his only remaining consolation. Of his two sons, he is deprived of one by the parricidal hands of his brother; the survivor is deservedly the object of his detestation and abhorrence.

Abel, cruelly assassinated in the flower of his age, exhibits an example of human calamity. Noah, while the whole world securely abandons itself to sensual delights, consumes a valuable part of his life with excessive fatigue in building the ark. His escape from death was attended with greater distress than if he had died a hundred times. For besides that the ark was, as it were, a sepulchre to him for ten months, nothing could be more disagreeable than to be detained for so long a period almost immersed in the ordure of animals. After having escaped from such great difficulties, he meets with a fresh occasion of grief. He sees himself ridiculed by his own son, and is constrained to pronounce a curse with his own mouth upon him, whom by the great goodness of God he had received safe from the deluge.

XI. Abraham is one who ought to be deemed equal to a host, if we consider his faith, which is proposed to us as the best standard of believing, so that we must be numbered in his family, in order to be the children of God. Now, what would be more absurd, than that Abraham should be the father of all the faithful, and not possess even the lowest place among them? But he cannot be excluded from the number, nor even from the most honourable station, without the destruction of the whole Church. Now, with respect to the circumstances of his life;—when he is first called, he is torn by the Divine command from his country, his parents, and his friends, the enjoyment of whom is supposed to give life its principal relish; as though God positively intended to deprive him of all the pleasures of life. As soon as he has entered the land in which he is commanded to reside, he is driven from it by a famine. He removes, in search of relief, to a place where, for the preservation of his own safety, he finds it necessary to disown his wife, which would probably be more afflictive to him than many deaths. After having returned to the country of his residence, he is again expelled from it by famine. What kind of felicity is it to dwell in such a country, where he must so frequently experience hunger, and even perish for want of sustenance, unless he leaves it? In the country of Abimelech, he is again driven to the same necessity of purchasing his own personal safety with the loss of his wife. While he wanders hither and thither for many years in an unsettled state, he is compelled, by the continual quarrels of his servants, to send away his nephew, whom he regarded as a son. There is no doubt that he bore this separation just as he would the amputation of one of his limbs. Soon after he is informed that enemies have carried him away captive. Whithersoever he directs his course, he finds himself surrounded by savage barbarians, who will not even permit him to drink the water of wells which with immense labour he has himself digged. For he could not have bought the use of them from the king of Gerar, if it had not been previously prohibited. When he arrives to old age, beyond the time of having children, he experiences the most disagreeable and painful circumstance with which that age is attended. He sees himself destitute of posterity, till, beyond all expectation, he begets Ishmael; whose birth he purchases at a dear rate, while he is wearied with the reproaches of Sarah, just as if he encouraged the contumacy of his maid-servant, and so were himself the cause of the domestic disturbance. At length Isaac is born; but his birth is attended with this condition, that Ishmael the first-born must be banished from the family, and abandoned like an enemy. When Isaac is left alone to solace the good man in his declining years, he is soon after commanded to sacrifice him. What can the human mind imagine more calamitous, than for a father to become the executioner of his own son? If he had been taken away by sickness, every one would have thought the aged parent unhappy in the extreme, as having had a son given him in mockery, at the loss of whom, his former grief on account of his being destitute of children would certainly be redoubled. If he had been massacred by some stranger, the calamity would have been greatly increased by the horrible nature of his end; but to be slain by his father's own hand exceeds all the other instances of distress. In short, through the whole course of his life, Abraham was so driven about and afflicted, that if any one wished to give an example of a life full of calamity, he could not find one more suitable. Nor let it be objected, that he was not entirely miserable, because he had at length a prosperous deliverance from such numerous and extreme dangers. For we cannot pronounce his to be a happy life, who for a long period struggles through an infinity of difficulties; but his, who is exempted from afflictions, and favoured with the peaceful enjoyment of present blessings.

XII. Isaac, though afflicted with fewer calamities, yet scarcely ever enjoys the smallest taste of pleasure. He also experiences those vexations which permit not a man to be happy in the world. Famine drives him from the land of Canaan; his wife is torn from his bosom; his neighbours frequently harass him, and take every method of distressing him, so that he also is constrained to contend with them about water. In his own family he suffers much uneasiness from Esau's wives; he is distressed by the discord of his sons, and unable to remedy that great evil, but by the exile of him to whom he had given the blessing. With respect to Jacob, he is an eminent example of nothing but extreme infelicity. He passes his childhood at home, amidst the menaces and terrors of his elder brother, to which he is at length constrained to give way. A fugitive from his parents and his native soil, in addition to the bitterness of exile, he is treated with unkindness by his uncle Laban. It is not sufficient for him to endure a most hard and severe servitude of seven years, but he is fraudulently deceived in a wife. For the sake of another wife he must enter on a new servitude, in which, as he himself complains, he is scorched all the day by the fervid rays of the sun, and through the wakeful night benumbed by the icy cold. During twenty years, which he spends in such extreme hardships, he is daily afflicted with fresh injuries from his father-in-law. Nor does he enjoy tranquillity in his own family, which he sees distracted and almost torn asunder by the animosities, contentions, and rivalship of his wives. When he is commanded to return to his own country, he is obliged to depart in a manner resembling an ignominious flight. Nor even then can he escape the iniquity of his father-in-law, but is harassed with his reproaches and insults in the midst of his journey. Immediately after, he falls into a much greater difficulty. For as he advances towards his brother, he has death before his eyes in as many forms as a cruel and inveterate enemy can possibly contrive. He is exceedingly tormented and distracted with dreadful terrors, while he is expecting the approach of his brother; when he sees him, he falls at his feet like a person half dead, till he finds him more reconciled than he could have ventured to hope. Moreover, on his first entrance into the land, he is deprived of Rachel, his dearly beloved wife. Afterwards he hears that the son whom he had by her, and whom, therefore, he loved above the rest, is torn asunder by wild beasts. The severity of his grief on account of his death is expressed by himself, when, after many days of mourning, he obstinately refuses all consolation, saying, "I will go down into the grave unto my son mourning." In the mean time, the rape and violation of his daughter, and the rashness of his sons in revenging it, which not only made him an object of abhorrence to all the inhabitants of the country, but put him in immediate danger of being massacred; what abundant sources were these of anxiety, grief, and vexation! Then follows the horrible crime of Reuben, his first-born, than which no greater affliction could befall him. For if the pollution of a man's wife be numbered among the greatest miseries, what shall we say of it, when the crime is perpetrated by his own son? Not long after, his family is contaminated with incest; so that such a number of disgraceful occurrences may be expected to break a heart otherwise very firm and unbroken by calamities. Towards the end of life, when he is seeking sustenance for himself and family in a season of famine, his ears are wounded by the report of a new calamity, which informs him that one of his sons is detained in prison; and in order to recover him he is obliged to intrust his darling Benjamin to the care of the rest. Who can suppose that in such an accumulation of distresses he had a single moment of respite? He himself, who is best able to give a testimony respecting himself, declares to Pharaoh, that his days on the earth have been few and evil. By affirming that he has lived in continual miseries, he denies that he has enjoyed that prosperity which the Lord had promised him. Therefore either Jacob formed an improper and ungrateful estimate of the favour of God, or he spake the truth in asserting that he had been miserable on the earth. If his affirmation was true, it follows that his hope was not fixed on terrestrial things.

XIII. If these holy fathers expected, as undoubtedly they did expect, a life of happiness from the hand of God, they both knew and contemplated a different kind of blessedness from that of this terrestrial life. This the apostle very beautifully shows, when he says, "By faith Abraham sojourned in the land of promise, as in a strange country, dwelling in tabernacles with Isaac and Jacob, the heirs with him of the same promise; for he looked for a city which hath foundations, whose builder and maker is God. These all died in faith, not having received the promises, but having seen them afar off, and were persuaded of them, and embraced them and confessed that they were strangers and pilgrims on the earth. For they that say such things declare plainly that they seek a country. And truly if they had been mindful of that country from whence they came out, they might have had opportunity to have returned. But now they desire a better country, that is, a heavenly; wherefore God is not ashamed to be called their God; for he hath prepared for them a city." For they would have been stupid beyond all comparison, so steadily to follow promises, of which there appeared no hope on earth, unless they had expected the completion of them in another world. But the apostle, with great force, principally insists on this—that they called the present life a pilgrimage, as is also stated by Moses. For if they were strangers and sojourners in the land of Canaan, what became of the Divine promise, by which they had been appointed heirs of it? This manifestly implies, therefore, that the promise, which the Lord had given them concerning the possession of it, related to something more remote. Wherefore they never acquired a foot of land in Canaan, except for a sepulchre; by which they testified that they had no hope of enjoying the benefit of the promise till after death. And this is the reason why Jacob thought it so exceedingly desirable to be buried there, that he made his son Joseph promise it to him by oath; and why Joseph commanded that his bones should be removed thither, even several ages after his death, when they would have been long reduced to ashes.

XIV. In short, it evidently appears, that in all the pursuits of life they kept in view the blessedness of the future state. For why should Jacob have so eagerly desired, and exposed himself to such danger in endeavouring to obtain, the primogeniture, which would occasion his exile, and almost his rejection from his family, but from which he could derive no possible benefit, unless he had his views fixed on a nobler blessing? And that such was his view he declared in these words, which he uttered with his expiring breath: "I have waited for thy salvation, O Lord." What salvation could he expect, when he felt himself about to expire, unless he had seen in death the commencement of a new life? But why do we argue concerning the saints and children of God, when even one, who in other respects endeavoured to oppose the truth, was not entirely destitute of such a knowledge? For what was the meaning of Balaam, when he said, "Let me die the death of the righteous, and let my last end be like his," but the same which David afterwards expressed in the following words? "Precious in the sight of the Lord is the death of his saints." "Evil shall slay the wicked." If death were the ultimate bound of human existence, no difference could be observed in it between the righteous and the impious; the distinction between them consists in the different destinies which await them after death.

XV. We have not yet proceeded beyond Moses; whose only office, our opponents allege, was to persuade a carnal people to the worship of God by the fertility of the land, and an abundance of all things: and yet, unless any one wilfully rejects the evidence presented to him, we already discover a clear declaration of a spiritual covenant. But if we come down to the prophets, there we have the fullest revelation both of eternal life and of the kingdom of Christ. And first, with what perspicuity and certainty does David direct all his writings to this end; though, as he was prior to the rest in point of time, so, according to the order of the Divine dispensation, he shadowed forth the heavenly mysteries more obscurely than they did! What estimate he formed of his terrestrial habitation, the following passage declares: "I am a stranger with thee, and a sojourner, as all my fathers were. Verily, every man at his best estate is altogether vanity. Surely every man walketh in a vain show. And now, Lord, what wait I for? my hope is in thee." He who, after having confessed that there is nothing substantial or permanent on earth, still retains the constancy of his hope in God, certainly contemplates the felicity reserved for him in another world. To this contemplation he frequently recalls the faithful, whenever he wishes to afford them true consolation. For in another place, after having spoken of the brevity and the transitory nature of human life, he adds, "But the mercy of the Lord is from everlasting to everlasting upon them that fear him." Similar to which is the following: "Of old hast thou laid the foundations of the earth; and the heavens are the work of thy hands. They shall perish, but thou shalt endure; yea, all of them shall wax old like a garment; as a vesture shalt thou change them, and they shall be changed; but thou art the same, and thy years shall have no end. The children of thy servants shall continue, and their seed shall be established before thee." If, notwithstanding the destruction of heaven and earth, the pious cease not to be established before the Lord, it follows that their salvation is connected with his eternity. But this hope cannot be at all supported, unless it rest on the promise which we find in Isaiah: "The heavens," saith the Lord, "shall vanish away like smoke, and the earth shall wax old like a garment, and they that dwell therein shall die in like manner; but my salvation shall be for ever, and my righteousness shall not be abolished;" where perpetuity is ascribed to righteousness and salvation, considered not as resident in God, but as experienced by men.

XVI. Nor can what he frequently says concerning the prosperity of the faithful be understood in any other sense than as referring to the manifestation of the glory of heaven. Such are the following passages: "The Lord preserveth the souls of his saints; he delivereth them out of the hand of the wicked. Light is sown for the righteous, and gladness for the upright in heart." Again: "The righteousness of the righteous endureth for ever; his horn shall be exalted with honour. The desire of the wicked shall perish." Again: "Surely the righteous shall give thanks unto thy name; the upright shall dwell in thy presence." Again: "The righteous shall be had in everlasting remembrance." Again: "The Lord redeemeth the soul of his servants." For the Lord frequently leaves his servants to the rage of the impious, not only to be harassed, but to be torn asunder and ruined; he suffers good men to languish in obscurity and meanness, while the impious are almost as glorious as the stars; nor does he exhilarate the faithful with the light of his countenance, so that they can enjoy any lasting pleasure. Wherefore David does not dissemble that, if the faithful fix their eyes on the present state of things, they will be most grievously tempted with an apprehension lest innocence should obtain from God neither favour nor reward. So much does impiety in most cases prosper and flourish, while the pious are oppressed with ignominy, poverty, contempt, and distress of every kind. "My feet," says he, "were almost gone; my steps had well nigh slipped. For I was envious at the foolish, when I saw the prosperity of the wicked." At length he concludes his account of them: "When I thought to know this, it was too painful for me; until I went into the sanctuary of God; then understood I their end."

XVII. We may learn, then, even from this confession of David, that the holy fathers under the Old Testament were not ignorant, that God rarely or never in this world gives his servants those things which he promises them, and that, therefore, they elevated their minds to the sanctuary of God, where they had a treasure in reserve which is not visible amid the shadows of the present life. This sanctuary was the last judgment, which, not being discernible by their eyes, they were contented to apprehend by faith. Relying on this confidence, whatever events might befall them in the world, they, nevertheless, had no doubt that there would come a time when the Divine promises would be fulfilled. This is evident from the following passages: "I will behold thy face in righteousness: I shall be satisfied, when I awake, with thy likeness." Again: "I am like a green olive-tree in the house of God." Again: "The righteous shall flourish like the palm-tree: he shall grow like a cedar in Lebanon. Those that be planted in the house of the Lord shall flourish in the courts of our God. They shall still bring forth fruit in old age; they shall be fat and flourishing." He had just before said, "O Lord, how great are thy works! and thy thoughts are very deep. When the wicked spring as the grass, and when all the workers of iniquity do flourish, it is that they shall be destroyed for ever." Where can this beauty and gracefulness of the faithful be found, but where the appearance of this world has been reversed by the manifestation of the kingdom of God? When they could turn their eyes towards that eternity, despising the momentary rigour of present calamities, they securely broke forth into the following expressions: "The Lord shall never suffer the righteous to be moved. But thou, O God, shalt bring them" (wicked men) "down into the pit of destruction." Where, in this world, is the pit of destruction, to absorb the wicked, as an instance of whose felicity it is mentioned in another place that without languishing for any long time "they go down to the grave in a moment?" Where is that great stability of the saints, whom David himself, in the language of complaint, frequently represents as not only troubled, but oppressed and consumed? He certainly had in view, not any thing that results from the agitations of the world, which are even more tumultuous than those of the sea, but what will be accomplished by the Lord, when he shall one day sit in judgment to fix the everlasting destiny of heaven and earth. This appears from another psalm, in which he gives the following beautiful description: "They that trust in their wealth, and boast themselves in the multitude of their riches; none of them can by any means redeem his brother, nor give to God a ransom for him. For he seeth that wise men die, likewise the fool and the brutish person perish, and leave their wealth to others. Their inward thought is, that their houses shall continue for ever, and their dwelling-places to all generations; they call their lands after their own names. Nevertheless man being in honour abideth not: he is like the beasts that perish. This their way is their folly: yet their posterity approve their sayings. Like sheep they are laid in the grave; death shall feed on them; and the upright shall have dominion over them in the morning; and their beauty shall consume in the grave from their dwelling." In the first place, this derision of fools, for placing their dependence on the mutable and transitory blessings of the world, shows that the wise ought to seek a very different felicity. But he more evidently discloses the mystery of the resurrection, when he establishes the reign of the pious after the ruin and destruction of the wicked. For what shall we understand by "the morning" which he mentions, but the revelation of a new life commencing after the conclusion of the present?

XVIII. Hence arose that reflection, which served the faithful as a consolation under their miseries, and a remedy for their sufferings: "The anger of the Lord endureth but a moment; in his favour is life." How did they limit their afflictions to a moment, who were afflicted all their lifetime? When did they perceive so long a duration of the Divine goodness, of which they had scarcely the smallest taste? If their views had been confined to the earth, they could have made no such discovery; but as they directed their eyes towards heaven, they perceived, that the afflictions with which the Lord exercises his saints are but "for a small moment," and that the "mercies" with which he "gathers" them are "everlasting." On the other hand, they foresaw the eternal and never-ending perdition of the impious, who had been happy, as in a dream, for a single day. Hence the following sentiments: "The memory of the just is blessed; but the name of the wicked shall rot." "Precious in the sight of the Lord is the death of his saints." Also in Samuel: "The Lord will keep the feet of his saints, and the wicked shall be silent in darkness." These expressions suggest to us, that they well knew, that whatever vicissitudes may befall the saints, yet their last end will be life and salvation; and that the prosperity of the impious is a pleasant path, which gradually leads to the gulf of everlasting death. Therefore they called the death of such the "destruction of the uncircumcised," as of those from whom all hope of resurrection had been cut off. Wherefore David could not conceive a more grievous imprecation than this: "Let them be blotted out of the book of the living, and not be written with the righteous."

XIX. But the following declaration of Job is remarkable beyond all others: "I know that my Redeemer liveth, and that he shall stand at the latter day upon the earth; and though after my skin, worms destroy this body, yet in my flesh shall I see God; whom I shall see for myself, and mine eyes shall behold, and not another." Some, who wish to display their critical sagacity, cavil that this is not to be understood of the final resurrection, but even of the first day on which Job expected God to be more propitious to him. Though we partly concede this, we shall extort an acknowledgment from them, whether they are willing or not, that Job could never have attained to such an enlarged hope, if his thoughts had been confined to the earth. We must, therefore, be obliged to confess that he, who saw that his Redeemer would be present with him even when lying in the sepulchre, must have elevated his views to a future immortality. For to them, who think only of the present life, death is a source of extreme despair, which, however, could not annihilate his hope. "Though he slay me," said he, "yet will I trust in him." Nor let any trifler here object, that these were the expressions of a few persons, and are far from furnishing proof that such a doctrine was current among the Jews. I will immediately reply, that these few persons did not in these declarations reveal any recondite wisdom, in which only superior understandings were separately and privately instructed; but that the Holy Spirit having constituted them teachers of the people, they publicly promulgated the Divine mysteries which were to be generally received, and to be the principles of the popular religion. When we hear the public oracles of the Holy Spirit, therefore, in which he has so clearly and evidently spoken of the spiritual life in the Jewish church, it would be intolerable perverseness to apply them entirely to the carnal covenant, in which no mention is made but of the earth and earthly opulence.

XX. If we descend to the later prophets, there we may freely expatiate as quite at home. For if it was not difficult to prove our point from David, Job, and Samuel, we shall do it there with much greater facility. For this is the order and economy which God observed in dispensing the covenant of his mercy, that as the course of time accelerated the period of its full exhibition, he illustrated it from day to day with additional revelations. Therefore, in the beginning, when the first promise was given to Adam, it was like the kindling of some feeble sparks. Subsequent accessions caused a considerable enlargement of the light, which continued to increase more and more, and diffused its splendour through a wide extent, till at length, every cloud being dissipated, Christ, the Sun of Righteousness, completely illuminated the whole world. There is no reason to fear, therefore, if we want the suffrages of the prophets in support of our cause, that they will fail us. But as I perceive it would be a very extensive field, which would engross more of our attention than the nature of our design will admit,—for it would furnish matter for a large volume,—and as I also think that by what has been already said, I have prepared the way even for a reader of small penetration to proceed without any difficulties, I shall abstain from a prolixity which at present is not very necessary. I shall only caution the reader to advance with the clew which we have put into his hand; namely, that whenever the prophets mention the blessedness of the faithful, scarcely any vestiges of which are discernible in the present life, he should recur to this distinction; that in order to the better elucidation of the Divine goodness, the prophets represented it to the people in a figurative manner; but that they gave such a representation of it as would withdraw the mind from earth and time, and the elements of this world, all which must ere long perish, and would necessarily excite to a contemplation of the felicity of the future spiritual life.

XXI. We will content ourselves with one example. When the Israelites, after being carried to Babylon, perceived how very much their dispersion resembled a death, they could scarcely be convinced that the prophecy of Ezekiel concerning their restitution was not a mere fable; for they considered it in the same light, as if he had announced, that putrid carcasses would be restored to life. The Lord, in order to show that even that difficulty would not prevent him from displaying his beneficence, gave the prophet a vision of a field full of dry bones, which he instantaneously restored to life and vigour solely by the power of his word. The vision served indeed to correct the existing incredulity; but at the same time it reminded the Jews, how far the power of the Lord extended beyond the restoration of the people, since the mere expression of his will so easily reanimated the dry and dispersed bones. Wherefore you may properly compare that passage with another of Isaiah: "Thy dead men shall live; together with my dead body shall they arise. Awake and sing, ye that dwell in dust; for thy dew is as the dew of herbs, and the earth shall cast out the dead. Come, my people, enter thou into thy chambers, and shut thy doors about thee: hide thyself as it were for a little moment, until the indignation be overpast. For, behold, the Lord cometh out of his place to punish the inhabitants of the earth for their iniquity: the earth also shall disclose her blood, and shall no more cover her slain."

XXII. It would be absurd, however, to attempt to reduce every passage to such a canon of interpretation. For there are some places, which show without any disguise the future immortality which awaits the faithful in the kingdom of God. Such are some which we have recited, and such are many others, but particularly these two; one in Isaiah: "As the new heavens and the new earth which I will make, shall remain before me, saith the Lord, so shall your seed and your name remain. And it shall come to pass, that from one new moon to another, and from one sabbath to another, shall all flesh come to worship before me, saith the Lord. And they shall go forth, and look upon the carcasses of the men that have transgressed against me; for their worm shall not die, neither shall their fire be quenched." And another in Daniel: "At that time shall Michael stand up, the great prince which standeth for the children of thy people; and there shall be a time of trouble such as never was since there was a nation even to that same time; and at that time thy people shall be delivered, every one that shall be found written in the book. And many of them that sleep in the dust of the earth shall awake, some to everlasting life, and some to shame and everlasting contempt."

XXIII. Now, the two remaining points, that the fathers had Christ as the pledge of their covenant, and that they reposed in him all their confidence of the blessing, being less controvertible and more plain, I shall take no pains to prove them. We may safely conclude, therefore, what all the machinations of the devil can never subvert, that the Old Testament, or covenant which the Lord made with the Israelitish nation, was not limited to terrestrial things, but contained a promise of spiritual and eternal life; the expectation of which must have been impressed on the minds of all who truly consented to the covenant. Then let us drive far away from us this absurd and pernicious notion, either that the Lord proposed nothing else to the Jews, or that the Jews sought nothing else, but an abundance of food, carnal delights, flourishing wealth, external power, a numerous offspring, and whatever is esteemed valuable by a natural man. For under the present dispensation, Christ promises to his people no other kingdom of heaven, than where they may sit down with Abraham, Isaac, and Jacob; and Peter asserted the Jews of his time to be heirs of the grace of the gospel, when he said that "they were the children of the prophets, and of the covenant which God made with their fathers." And that this might not only be testified in words, the Lord also proved it by a matter of fact. For on the day in which he rose from the dead, he honoured many of the saints with a participation of his resurrection, and caused them to appear in the city; thus furnishing a certain assurance that whatever he did and suffered for the acquisition of eternal salvation, belonged to the faithful of the Old Testament as much as to us. For, as Peter declares, they also were endued with the same Spirit, who is the author of our regeneration to life. When we are informed that the same Spirit, which is as it were a spark of immortality in us, and is therefore called in one place "the earnest of our inheritance," dwelt in a similar manner in them, how can we dare to deprive them of the inheritance of eternal life? It is therefore the more surprising, that the Sadducees formerly fell into such stupidity as to deny the resurrection, and the immortality of the soul, since they had proofs of these points from such clear testimonies of Scripture. And the folly of the whole nation of the Jews in the present age, in expecting an earthly kingdom of the Messiah, would be equally extraordinary, had not the Scriptures long before predicted that they would thus be punished for their rejection of the gospel. For it was consistent with the righteous judgment of God to strike with blindness the minds of those, who, rejecting the light of heaven when presented to them, kept themselves in voluntary darkness. Therefore they read Moses, and assiduously turn over his pages, but are prevented by an interposing veil from perceiving the light which beams in his countenance; and thus it will remain covered and concealed to them, till they are converted to Christ, from whom they now endeavour as much as they can to withdraw and divert it.

5. THE DIFFERENCE OF THE TWO TESTAMENTS.

What, then, it will be said, will there be no difference left between the Old Testament and the New? and what becomes of all those passages of Scripture, where they are compared together as things that are very different? I readily admit the differences which are mentioned in the Scripture, but I maintain that they derogate nothing from the unity already established; as will be seen when we have discussed them in proper order. But the principal differences, as far as my observation or memory extends, are four in number; to which if any one choose to add a fifth, I shall not make the least objection. I assert, and engage to demonstrate, that all these are such as pertain rather to the mode of administration, than to the substance. In this view, they will not prevent the promises of the Old and New Testament from remaining the same, and the promises of both Testaments from having in Christ the same foundation. Now, the first difference is, that although it was always the will of the Lord that the minds of his people should be directed, and their hearts elevated, towards the celestial inheritance, yet, in order that they might be the better encouraged to hope for it, he anciently exhibited it for their contemplation and partial enjoyment under the figures of terrestrial blessings. Now, having by the gospel more clearly and explicitly revealed the grace of the future life, he leaves the inferior mode of instruction which he used with the Israelites, and directs our minds to the immediate contemplation of it. Those who overlook this design of God, suppose that the ancients ascended no higher than the corporeal blessings which were promised them; they so frequently hear the land of Canaan mentioned as the eminent, and indeed the only, reward for the observers of the Divine law. They hear that God threatens the transgressors of this law with nothing more severe than being expelled from the possession of that country, and dispersed into foreign lands. They see this to be nearly the whole substance of all the blessings and of all the curses pronounced by Moses. Hence they confidently conclude, that the Jews were separated from other nations, not for their own sakes, but for ours, that the Christian Church might have an image, in whose external form they could discern examples of spiritual things. But since the Scripture frequently shows, that God himself appointed the terrestrial advantages with which he favoured them for the express purpose of leading them to the hope of celestial blessings, it argued extreme inexperience, not to say stupidity, not to consider such a dispensation. The point of controversy between us and these persons, is this: they maintain that the possession of the land of Canaan was accounted by the Israelites their supreme and ultimate blessedness, but that to us, since the revelation of Christ, it is a figure of the heavenly inheritance. We, on the contrary, contend, that in the earthly possession which they enjoyed, they contemplated, as in a mirror, the future inheritance which they believed to be prepared for them in heaven.

II. This will more fully appear from the similitude which Paul has used in his Epistle to the Galatians. He compares the Jewish nation to a young heir, who, being yet incapable of governing himself, follows the dictates of a tutor or a governor, to whose charge he has been committed. His application of this similitude chiefly to the ceremonies, is no objection against the propriety of its application to our present purpose. The same inheritance was destined for them as for us; but they were not of a sufficient age to be capable of entering on the possession and management of it. The Church among them was the same as among us; but it was yet in a state of childhood. Therefore the Lord kept them under this tuition, that he might give them the spiritual promises, not open and unconcealed, but veiled under terrestrial figures. Therefore, when he admitted Abraham, Isaac, and Jacob, with their posterity, to the hope of immortality, he promised them the land of Canaan as their inheritance; not that their hopes might terminate in that land, but that in the prospect of it they might exercise and confirm themselves in the hope of that true inheritance which was not yet visible. And that they might not be deceived, a superior promise was given them, which proved that country not to be the highest blessing which God would bestow. Thus Abraham is not permitted to grow indolent after having received a promise of the land, but a greater promise elevates his mind to the Lord. For he hears him saying, "Abram, I am thy shield, and thy exceeding great reward." Here we see that the Lord proposes himself to Abraham as his ultimate reward, that he may not seek an uncertain and transitory one in the elements of this world, but may consider that which can never fade away. God afterwards annexes a promise of the land, merely as a symbol of his benevolence, and a type of the heavenly inheritance. And that this was the opinion of the saints, is plain from their own language. Thus David rises from temporary blessings to that consummate and ultimate felicity. "My soul longeth, yea, even fainteth, for the courts of the Lord." "God is my portion for ever." Again: "The Lord is the portion of mine inheritance and of my cup: thou maintainest my lot." Again: "I cried unto thee, O Lord: I said, Thou art my refuge and my portion in the land of the living." Persons who venture to express themselves thus, certainly profess that in their hopes they rise above the world and all present blessings. Nevertheless the prophets frequently describe this blessedness of the future world under the type which the Lord had given them. In this sense we must understand the following passages: "The righteous shall inherit the land;" "But the wicked shall be cut off from the earth;" and various predictions of Isaiah, which foretell the future prosperity of Jerusalem, and the abundance that will be enjoyed in Zion. We see that all these things are inapplicable to the land of our pilgrimage, or to the earthly Jerusalem, but that they belong to the true country of the faithful, and to that celestial city, where "the Lord commanded the blessing, even life for evermore."

III. This is the reason why the saints, under the Old Testament, are represented as holding this mortal life with its blessings in higher estimation than becomes us now. For although they well knew that they ought not to rest in it as the end of their course, yet when they recollected what characters of his grace the Lord had impressed on it, in order to instruct them in a manner suitable to their tender state, they felt a greater degree of pleasure in it than if they had considered it merely in itself. But as the Lord, in declaring his benevolence to the faithful by present blessings, gave them, under these types and symbols, a figurative exhibition of spiritual felicity, so, on the other hand, in corporal punishments he exemplified his judgment against the reprobate. Therefore, as the favours of God were more conspicuous in earthly things, so also were his punishments. Injudicious persons, not considering this analogy and harmony (so to speak) between the punishments and rewards, wonder at so great a variety in God, that in ancient times he was ready to avenge all the transgressions of men by the immediate infliction of severe and dreadful punishments, but now, as if he had laid aside his ancient wrath, punishes with far less severity and frequency; and on this account they almost adopt the notion of the Manichæans, that the God of the Old Testament is a different being from the God of the New. But we shall easily get rid of such difficulties, if we direct our attention to that dispensation of God, which I have observed; namely, that during that period, in which he gave the Israelites his covenant involved in some degree of obscurity, he intended to signify and prefigure the grace of future and eternal felicity by terrestrial blessings, and the grievousness of spiritual death by corporal punishments.

IV. Another difference between the Old Testament and the New consists in figures, because the former, in the absence of the truth, displayed merely an image and shadow instead of the body; but the latter exhibits the present truth and the substantial body. And this is generally mentioned wherever the New Testament is opposed to the Old, but is treated more at large in the Epistle to the Hebrews than in any other place. The apostle is there disputing against those who supposed that the observance of the Mosaic law could not be abolished, without being followed by the total ruin of religion. To refute this error, he adduces the prediction of the psalmist concerning the priesthood of Christ; for since he has an eternal priesthood committed to him, we may argue the certain abolition of that priesthood, in which new priests daily succeeded each other. But he proves the superiority of the appointment of this new Priest, because it is confirmed with an oath. He afterwards adds that this transfer of the priesthood implies also a change of the covenant. And he proves that this change was necessary, because such was the imbecility of the law, that it could bring nothing to perfection. Then he proceeds to state the nature of this imbecility; namely, that the law prescribed external righteousnesses, consisting in carnal ordinances, which could not make the observers of them "perfect as pertaining to the conscience," that by animal victims it could neither expiate sins nor procure true holiness. He concludes, therefore, that it contained "a shadow of good things to come, but not the very image of the things;" and that consequently it had no other office, but to serve as an introduction to "a better hope," which is exhibited in the gospel. Here we have to inquire in what respect the Legal covenant is compared with the Evangelical, the ministry of Christ with the ministry of Moses. For if the comparison related to the substance of the promises, there would be a great discordance between the two testaments; but as the state of the question leads us to a different point, we must attend to the scope of the apostle, in order to discover the truth. Let us, then, bring forward the covenant, which God has once made, which is eternal, and never to be abolished. The accomplishment, whence it derives its establishment and ratification, is Christ. While such a confirmation was waited for, the Lord by Moses prescribed ceremonies, to serve as solemn symbols of the confirmation. It came to be a subject of contention, whether the ceremonies ordained in the law ought to cease and give place to Christ. Now, though these ceremonies were only accidents or concomitants of the covenant, yet being the instruments of its administration, they bear the name of the covenant; as it is common to give to other sacraments the names of the things they represent. In a word, therefore, what is here called the Old Testament is a solemn method of confirming the covenant, consisting of ceremonies and sacrifices. Since it contains nothing substantial, unless we proceed further, the apostle contends that it ought to be repealed and abrogated, in order to make way for Christ, the Surety and Mediator of a better testament, by whom eternal sanctification has been at once procured for the elect, and those transgressions obliterated, which remained under the law. Or, if you prefer it, take the following statement of it; that the Old Testament of the Lord was that which was delivered to the Jews, involved in a shadowy and inefficacious observance of ceremonies, and that it was therefore temporary, because it remained as it were in suspense, till it was supported by a firm and substantial confirmation; but that it was made new and eternal, when it was consecrated and established by the blood of Christ. Whence Christ calls the cup which he gives to his disciples in the supper, "the cup of the New Testament in his blood;" to signify that when the testament of God is sealed with his blood, the truth of it is then accomplished, and thus it is made new and eternal.

V. Hence it appears in what sense the apostle said, that the Jews were conducted to Christ by the tuition of the law, before he was manifested in the flesh. He confesses also that they were children and heirs of God, but such as, on account of their age, required to be kept under the care of a tutor. For it was reasonable that before the Sun of Righteousness was risen, there should be neither such a full blaze of revelation, nor such great clearness of understanding. Therefore the Lord dispensed the light of his word to them in such a manner, that they had yet only a distant and obscure prospect of it. Paul describes this slenderness of understanding as a state of childhood, which it was the Lord's will to exercise in the elements of this world and in external observances, as rules of puerile discipline, till the manifestation of Christ, by whom the knowledge of the faithful was to grow to maturity. Christ himself alluded to this distinction, when he said, "The law and the prophets were until John: since that time the kingdom of God is preached." What discoveries did Moses and the prophets make to their contemporaries? They afforded them some taste of that wisdom which was in after times to be clearly manifested, and gave them a distant prospect of its future splendour. But when Christ could be plainly pointed out, the kingdom of God was revealed. For in him are discovered "all the treasures of wisdom and knowledge," by which we penetrate almost into the furthest recesses of heaven.

VI. Nor is it any objection to our argument, that scarcely a person can be found in the Christian Church, who is to be compared with Abraham in the excellency of his faith; or that the prophets were distinguished by such energy of the Spirit as, even at this day, is sufficient to illuminate the whole world. For our present inquiry is, not what grace the Lord has conferred on a few, but what is the ordinary method which he has pursued in the instruction of his people; such as is found even among the prophets themselves, who were endued with peculiar knowledge above others. For their preaching is obscure, as relating to things very distant, and is comprehended in types. Besides, notwithstanding their wonderful eminence in knowledge, yet because they were under a necessity of submitting to the same tuition as the rest of the people, they are considered as sustaining the character of children as well as others. Finally, none of them possessed knowledge so clear as not to partake more or less of the obscurity of the age. Whence this observation of Christ: "Many prophets and kings have desired to see those things which ye see, and have not seen them; and to hear those things which ye hear, and have not heard them." "Blessed are your eyes, for they see; and your ears, for they hear." And, indeed, it is reasonable that the presence of Christ should be distinguished by the prerogative of introducing a clearer revelation of the mysteries of heaven. To the same purpose also is the passage, which we have before cited from the First Epistle of Peter, that it was revealed to them, that the principal advantage of their labours would be experienced in our times.

VII. I come now to the third difference, which is taken from Jeremiah, whose words are these: "Behold, the days come, saith the Lord, that I will make a new covenant with the house of Israel, and with the house of Judah; not according to the covenant that I made with their fathers in the day that I took them by the hand to bring them out of the land of Egypt; which my covenant they brake, although I was a husband to them, saith the Lord; but this shall be the covenant that I will make with the house of Israel. After those days, saith the Lord, I will put my law in their inward parts, and write it in their hearts; and will be their God, and they shall be my people. And they shall teach no more every man his neighbour, and every man his brother, saying, Know the Lord; for they shall all know me, from the least of them unto the greatest of them, saith the Lord; for I will forgive their iniquity, and I will remember their sin no more." From this passage the apostle took occasion to institute the following comparison between the law and the gospel: he calls the former a literal, the latter a spiritual doctrine; the former, he says, was engraven on tables of stone, but the latter is inscribed on the heart; the former was the preaching of death, but the latter of life; the former was the ministration of condemnation, but the latter of righteousness; the former is abolished, but the latter remains. As the design of the apostle was to express the sense of the prophet, it will be sufficient for us to consider the language of one of them, in order to discover the meaning of both. There is, however, some difference between them. For the apostle speaks of the law in less honourable terms than the prophet does; and that not simply with respect to the law itself, but, because there were some disturbers, who were full of improper zeal for the law, and by their perverse attachment to the ceremonies obscured the glory of the gospel, he disputes concerning the nature of the law with reference to their error and foolish affection for it. This peculiarity in Paul, therefore, will be worthy of our observation. Both of them, as they contrast the Old and New Testaments with each other, consider nothing in the law, but what properly belongs to it. For example, the law contains frequent promises of mercy; but as they are borrowed from another dispensation, they are not considered as part of the law, when the mere nature of the law is the subject of discussion. All that they attribute to it is, that it enjoins what is right, and prohibits crimes; that it proclaims a reward for the followers of righteousness, and denounces punishments against transgressors; but that it neither changes nor corrects the depravity of heart which is natural to all men.

VIII. Now, let us explain the comparison of the apostle in all its branches. In the first place, the Old Testament is literal, because it was promulgated without the efficacy of the Spirit; the New is spiritual, because the Lord has engraven it in a spiritual manner on the hearts of men. The second contrast, therefore, serves as an elucidation of the first. The Old Testament is the revelation of death, because it can only involve all mankind in a curse; the New is the instrument of life, because it delivers us from the curse, and restores us to favour with God. The former is the ministry of condemnation, because it convicts all the children of Adam of unrighteousness; the latter is the ministry of righteousness, because it reveals the mercy of God, by which we are made righteous. The last contrast must be referred to the legal ceremonies. The law having an image of things that were at a distance, it was necessary that in time it should be abolished and disappear. The gospel, exhibiting the body itself, retains a firm and perpetual stability. Jeremiah calls even the moral law a weak and frail covenant, but for another reason; namely, because it was soon broken by the sudden defection of an ungrateful people. But as such a violation arises from the fault of the people, it cannot be properly attributed to the Testament. The ceremonies, however, which at the advent of Christ were abolished by their own weakness, contained in themselves the cause of their abrogation. Now, this difference between the "letter" and the "spirit" is not to be understood as if the Lord had given his law to the Jews without any beneficial result, without one of them being converted to him; but it is used in a way of comparison, to display the plenitude of grace with which the same Legislator, assuming as it were a new character, has honoured the preaching of the gospel. For if we survey the multitude of those, from among all nations, whom, by the influence of his Spirit in the preaching of the gospel, the Lord has regenerated and gathered into communion with his Church, we shall say that those of the ancient Israelites, who cordially and sincerely embraced the covenant of the Lord, were extremely few; though, if estimated by themselves without any comparison, they amounted to a considerable number.

IX. The fourth difference arises out of the third. For the Scripture calls the Old Testament a covenant of bondage, because it produces fear in the mind; but the New it describes as a covenant of liberty, because it leads the heart to confidence and security. Thus Paul, in the eighth chapter of his Epistle to the Romans, says, "Ye have not received the spirit of bondage again to fear; but ye have received the Spirit of adoption, whereby we cry, Abba, Father." To the same purpose is that passage in the Epistle to the Hebrews, that the faithful now "are not come unto the mount that might be touched, and that burned with fire, nor unto blackness, and darkness, and tempest," where nothing can be either heard or seen, but what must strike terror into the mind; so that even Moses himself is exceedingly afraid at the sound of the terrible voice, which they all pray that they may hear no more; but that now the faithful "are come unto mount Sion, and unto the city of the living God, the heavenly Jerusalem," &c. What Paul briefly touches in the passage which we have adduced from the Epistle to the Romans, he explains more at large in his Epistle to the Galatians, when he allegorizes the two sons of Abraham in the following manner—that Agar, the bond-woman, is a type of mount Sinai, where the people of Israel received the law; that Sarah, the free-woman, is a figure of the celestial Jerusalem, whence proceeds the gospel. That as the son of Agar is born in bondage, and can never attain to the inheritance, and the son of Sarah is born free, and has a right to the inheritance, so by the law we were devoted to slavery, but by the gospel alone are regenerated to liberty. Now, the whole may be summed up thus—that the Old Testament filled men's consciences with fear and trembling; but that by the benefit of the New Testament, they are delivered, and enabled to rejoice. The former kept their consciences under a yoke of severe bondage; but by the liberality of the latter they are emancipated and admitted to liberty. If any one object to us the case of the holy fathers of the Israelitish people, that as they were clearly possessed of the same spirit of faith as we are, they must consequently have been partakers of the same liberty and joy, we reply, that neither of these originated from the law; but that, when they felt themselves, by means of the law, oppressed with their servile condition, and wearied with disquietude of conscience, they fled for refuge to the gospel; and that therefore it was a peculiar advantage of the New Testament, that they enjoyed an exception from the common law of the Old Testament, and were exempted from those evils. Besides, we shall deny that they were favoured with the spirit of liberty and security, to such a degree as not to experience from the law some measure both of fear and of servitude. For notwithstanding their enjoyment of that privilege, which they obtained by the grace of the gospel, yet they were subject to the same observances and burdens as the people in general. As they were obliged, therefore, to a diligent observance of these ceremonies, which were emblems of the state of pupilage similar to bondage, and the hand-writing, by which they confessed themselves guilty of sin, did not release them from the obligation, they may justly be said, in comparison with us, to have been under a testament of bondage and fear, when we consider the common mode of procedure which the Lord then pursued with the Israelitish nation.

X. The three last comparisons which we have mentioned are between the law and the gospel. In these, therefore, "the Old Testament" denotes the law; and "the New Testament," the gospel. The first comparison extends further, for it comprehends also the promises, which were given before the law. When Augustine denied that they ought to be considered as part of the Old Testament, he gave a very proper opinion, and intended the same that we now teach; for he had in view those passages of Jeremiah and Paul, in which the Old Testament is distinguished from the word of grace and mercy. He very judiciously adds also in the same place, that the children of the promise, from the beginning of the world, who have been regenerated by God, and, under the influence of faith working by love, have obeyed his commands, belong to the New Testament; and that, in hope, not of carnal, terrestrial, and temporal things, but of spiritual, celestial, and eternal blessings; especially believing in the Mediator, through whom they doubted not that the Spirit was dispensed to them to enable them to do their duty, and that whenever they sinned they were pardoned. For this is the very same thing which I meant to assert: That all the saints, whom, from the beginning of the world, the Scripture mentions as having been peculiarly chosen by God, have been partakers of the same blessing with us to eternal salvation. Between our distinction and that of Augustine there is this difference—that ours (according to this declaration of Christ, "the law and the prophets were until John; since that time the kingdom of God is preached;") distinguishes between the clearness of the gospel and the more obscure dispensation of the word which preceded it; whilst the other merely discriminates the weakness of the law from the stability of the gospel. Here it must also be remarked concerning the holy fathers, that though they lived under the Old Testament, they did not rest satisfied with it, but always aspired after the New, and thus enjoyed a certain participation of it. For all those who contented themselves with present shadows, and did not extend their views to Christ, are condemned by the apostle as blind and under the curse. For, to say nothing on other points, what greater ignorance can be imagined than to hope for an expiation of sin by the sacrifice of an animal? than to seek for the purification of the soul by an external ablution with water? than to wish to appease God with frigid ceremonies, as though they afforded him great pleasure? For all these absurdities are chargeable on those who adhere to the observances of the law, without any reference to Christ.

XI. The fifth difference, which we may add, consists in this—that till the advent of Christ, the Lord selected one nation, to which he would limit the covenant of his grace. Moses says, "When the Most High divided to the nations their inheritance, when he separated the sons of Adam,—the Lord's portion is his people; Jacob is the lot of his inheritance." In another place he thus addresses the people: "Behold, the heaven, and the heaven of heavens is the Lord's thy God, the earth also, with all that therein is. Only the Lord had a delight in thy fathers to love them, and he chose their seed after them, even you above all people." Therefore he favoured that people with the exclusive knowledge of his name, as though they alone of all mankind belonged to him; he deposited his covenant as it were in their bosom; to them he manifested the presence of his power; he honoured them with every privilege. But to omit the rest of his benefits, the only one that relates to our present argument is, that he united them to himself by the communication of his word, in order that he might be denominated and esteemed their God. In the mean time he suffered other nations, as though they had no business or intercourse with him, to walk in vanity; nor did he employ means to prevent their destruction by sending them the only remedy—the preaching of his word. The Israelitish nation, therefore, were then as darling sons; others were strangers: they were known to him, and received under his faithful protection; others were left to their own darkness: they were sanctified by God; others were profane: they were honoured with the Divine presence; others were excluded from approaching it. But when the fulness of the time was come, appointed for the restoration of all things, and the Reconciler of God and men was manifested, the barrier was demolished, which had so long confined the Divine mercy within the limits of the Jewish church, and peace was announced to them who were at a distance, and to them who were near, that being both reconciled to God, they might coalesce into one people. Wherefore "there is neither Greek nor Jew, circumcision nor uncircumcision, but Christ is all and in all;" "to whom the heathen are given for his inheritance, and the uttermost parts of the earth for his possession;" that he may have a universal "dominion from sea to sea, and from the river unto the ends of the earth."

XII. The vocation of the Gentiles, therefore, is an eminent illustration of the superior excellence of the New Testament above the Old. It had, indeed, before been most explicitly announced in numerous predictions of the prophets; but so as that the completion of it was deferred to the kingdom of the Messiah. And even Christ himself made no advances towards it at the first commencement of his preaching, but deferred it till he should have completed all the parts of our redemption, finished the time of his humiliation, and received from the Father "a name which is above every name, before which every knee shall bow." Wherefore, when this season was not yet arrived, he said to a Canaanitish woman, "I am not sent but unto the lost sheep of the house of Israel:" nor did he permit the apostles, in his first mission of them, to exceed these limits. "Go not," says he, "into the way of the Gentiles, and into any city of the Samaritans enter ye not; but go rather to the lost sheep of the house of Israel." And though this calling of the Gentiles was announced by so many testimonies, yet when the apostles were about to enter upon it, it appeared to them so novel and strange, that they dreaded it, as if it had been a prodigy: indeed it was with trepidation and reluctance that they at length engaged in it. Nor is this surprising; for it seemed not at all reasonable, that the Lord, who for so many ages had separated the Israelites from the rest of the nations, should, as it were, suddenly change his design, and annihilate this distinction. It had indeed been predicted in the prophecies; but they could not pay such great attention to the prophecies, as to be wholly unmoved with the novelty of the circumstance, which forced itself on their observation. Nor were the specimens, which the Lord had formerly given, of the future vocation of the Gentiles, sufficient to influence them. For besides his having called only very few of them, he had even incorporated them into the family of Abraham, that they might be added to his people; but by that public vocation, the Gentiles were not only raised to an equality with the Jews, but appeared to succeed to their places as though they had been dead. Besides, of all the strangers whom God had before incorporated into the Church, none were ever placed on an equality with the Jews. Therefore it is not without reason that Paul so celebrates this "mystery which was hidden from ages and from generations," and which he represents as an object of admiration even to angels.

XIII. In these four or five points, I think I have given a correct and faithful statement of the whole of the difference between the Old and the New Testament, as far as is sufficient for a simple system of doctrine. But because some persons represent this variety in the government of the Church, these different modes of instruction, and such a considerable alteration of rites and ceremonies, as a great absurdity, we must reply to them, before we proceed to other subjects. And this may be done in a brief manner, since the objections are not so strong as to require a laborious refutation. It is not reasonable, they say, that God, who is perpetually consistent with himself, should undergo so great a change as afterwards to disallow what he had once enjoined and commanded. I reply, that God ought not therefore to be deemed mutable, because he has accommodated different forms to different ages, as he knew would be suitable for each. If the husbandman prescribes different employments to his family in the winter, from those which he allots them in the summer, we must not therefore accuse him of inconstancy, or impute to him a deviation from the proper rules of agriculture, which are connected with the perpetual course of nature. Thus, also, if a father instructs, governs, and manages his children one way in infancy, another in childhood, and another in youth, we must not therefore charge him with being inconstant, or forsaking his own designs. Why, then, do we stigmatize God with the character of inconstancy, because he has made an apt and suitable distinction between different times? The last similitude ought fully to satisfy us. Paul compares the Jews to children, and Christians to youths. What impropriety is there in this part of the government of God, that he detained them in the rudiments which were suitable to them on account of their age, but has placed us under a stronger and more manly discipline? It is a proof, therefore, of the constancy of God, that he has delivered the same doctrine in all ages, and perseveres in requiring the same worship of his name which he commanded from the beginning. By changing the external form and mode, he has discovered no mutability in himself, but has so far accommodated himself to the capacity of men, which is various and mutable.

XIV. But they inquire whence this diversity proceeded, except from the will of God. Could he not, as well from the beginning as since the advent of Christ, give a revelation of eternal life in clear language without any figures, instruct his people by a few plain sacraments, bestow his Holy Spirit, and diffuse his grace through all the world? This is just the same as if they were to quarrel with God, because he created the world at so late a period, whereas he might have done it before; or because he has appointed the alternate vicissitudes of summer and winter, of day and night. But let us not doubt what ought to be believed by all pious men, that whatever is done by God is done wisely and righteously; although we frequently know nothing of the causes which render such transactions necessary. For it would be arrogating too much to ourselves, not to permit God to keep the reasons of his decrees concealed from us. But it is surprising, say they, that he now rejects and abominates the sacrifices of cattle, and all the apparatus of the Levitical priesthood, with which he used to be delighted; as though truly these external and transitory things could afford pleasure to God, or affect him in any way whatever. It has already been observed, that he did none of these things on his own account, but appointed them all for the salvation of men. If a physician cure a young man of any disease by a very excellent method, and afterwards adopt a different mode of cure with the same person when advanced in years, shall we therefore say that he rejects the method of cure which he before approved? We will rather say, that he perseveres in the same system, and considers the difference of age. Thus it was necessary, before the appearance of Christ, that he should be prefigured, and his future advent announced by one kind of emblems; since he has been manifested, it is right that he should be represented by others. But with respect to the Divine vocation, now more widely extended among all nations since the advent of Christ than it was before, and with regard to the more copious effusion of the graces of the Spirit, who can deny, that it is reasonable and just for God to retain under his own power and will the free dispensation of his favours; that he may illuminate what nations he pleases; that wherever he pleases he may introduce the preaching of his word; that he may give to his instruction whatever kind and degree of profit and success he pleases; that wherever he pleases, in any age, he may punish the ingratitude of the world by depriving them of the knowledge of his name, and when he pleases restore it on account of his mercy? We see, therefore, the absurdity of the cavils with which impious men disturb the minds of the simple on this subject, to call in question either the righteousness of God or the truth of the Scripture.

6. THE NECESSITY OF CHRIST BECOMING MAN IN ORDER TO FULFIL THE OFFICE OF MEDIATOR.

It was of great importance to our interests, that he, who was to be our Mediator, should be both true God and true man. If an inquiry be made concerning the necessity of this, it was not indeed a simple, or, as we commonly say, an absolute necessity, but such as arose from the heavenly decree, on which the salvation of men depended. But our most merciful Father has appointed that which was best for us. For since our iniquities, like a cloud intervening between us and him, had entirely alienated us from the kingdom of heaven, no one that could not approach to God could be a mediator for the restoration of peace. But who could have approached to him? Could any one of the children of Adam? They, with their parent, all dreaded the Divine presence. Could any one of the angels? They also stood in need of a head, by a connection with whom they might be confirmed in a perfect and unvarying adherence to their God. What, then, could be done? Our situation was truly deplorable, unless the Divine majesty itself would descend to us; for we could not ascend to it. Thus it was necessary that the Son of God should become Immanuel, that is, God with us; and this in order that there might be a mutual union and coalition between his Divinity and the nature of man; for otherwise the proximity could not be sufficiently near, nor could the affinity be sufficiently strong, to authorize us to hope that God would dwell with us. So great was the discordance between our pollution and the perfect purity of God. Although man had remained immaculately innocent, yet his condition would have been too mean for him to approach to God without a Mediator. What, then, can he do, after having been plunged by his fatal fall into death and hell, defiled with so many blemishes, putrefying in his own corruption, and, in a word, overwhelmed with every curse? It is not without reason, therefore, that Paul, when about to exhibit Christ in the character of a Mediator, expressly speaks of him as a man. "There is one Mediator," he says, "between God and man, the man Christ Jesus." He might have called him God, or might indeed have omitted the appellation of man, as well as that of God; but because the Spirit, who spake by him, knew our infirmity, he has provided a very suitable remedy against it, by placing the Son of God familiarly among us, as though he were one of us. Therefore, that no one may distress himself where he is to seek the Mediator, or in what way he may approach him, the apostle, by denominating him a man, apprizes us that he is near, and even close to us, since he is our own flesh. He certainly intends the same as is stated in another place more at large—"that we have not a high priest which cannot be touched with the feeling of our infirmities, but was in all points tempted like as we are, yet without sin."

II. This will still more fully appear, if we consider, that it was no mean part which the Mediator had to perform; namely, to restore us to the Divine favour, so as, of children of men, to make us children of God; of heirs of hell, to make us heirs of the kingdom of heaven. Who could accomplish this, unless the Son of God should become also the Son of man, and thus receive to himself what belongs to us, and transfer to us that which is his, and make that which is his by nature ours by grace? Depending, therefore, on this pledge, we have confidence that we are the children from God, because he, who is the Son of God by nature, has provided himself a body from our body, flesh from our flesh, bones from our bones, that he might be the same with us: he refused not to assume that which was peculiar to us, that we also might obtain that which he had peculiar to him; and that so in common with us he might be both the Son of God and the Son of man. Hence arises that holy fraternity, which he mentions with his own mouth in the following words: "I ascend unto my Father, and your Father; and to my God, and your God." On this account we have a certainty of the inheritance of the kingdom of heaven, because the only Son of God, to whom it exclusively belonged, has adopted us as his brethren; and if we are his brethren, we are consequently co-heirs to the inheritance. Moreover it was highly necessary also for this reason, that he who was to be our Redeemer should be truly both God and man. It was his office to swallow up death; who could do this, but he who was life itself? It was his to overcome sin; who could accomplish this, but righteousness itself? It was his to put to flight the powers of the world and of the air; who could do this, but a power superior both to the world and to the air? Now, who possesses life or righteousness, or the empire and power of heaven, but God alone? Therefore the most merciful God, when he determined on our redemption, became himself our Redeemer in the person of his only begotten Son!

III. Another branch of our reconciliation with God was this—that man, who had ruined himself by his own disobedience, should remedy his condition by obedience, should satisfy the justice of God, and suffer the punishment of his sin. Our Lord then made his appearance as a real man; he put on the character of Adam, and assumed his name, to act as his substitute in his obedience to the Father, to lay down our flesh as the price of satisfaction to the justice of God; and to suffer the punishment which we had deserved, in the same nature in which the offence had been committed. As it would have been impossible, therefore, for one who was only God to suffer death, or for one who was a mere man to overcome it, he associated the human nature with the Divine, that he might submit the weakness of the former to death, as an atonement for sins; and that with the power of the latter he might contend with death, and obtain a victory on our behalf. Those who despoil Christ, therefore, either of his Divinity or his humanity, either diminish his majesty and glory, or obscure his goodness. Nor are they, on the other hand, less injurious to men, whose faith they weaken and subvert; since it cannot stand any longer than it rests upon this foundation. Moreover, the Redeemer to be expected was that Son of Abraham and David, whom God had promised in the law and the prophets. Hence the minds of the faithful derive another advantage, because from the circumstance of his ancestry being traced to David and to Abraham, they have an additional assurance that this is the Christ, who was celebrated in so many prophecies. But we should particularly remember, what I have just stated—that our common nature is a pledge of our fellowship with the Son of God; that, clothed in our flesh, he vanquished sin and death, in order that the victory and triumph might be ours; that the flesh which he received from us he offered up as a sacrifice, in order to expiate and obliterate our guilt, and appease the just wrath of the Father.

IV. The persons who consider these things, with the diligent attention which they deserve, will easily disregard vague speculations which attract minds that are inconstant and fond of novelty. Such is the notion, that Christ would have become man, even though the human race had needed no redemption. I grant, indeed, that at the original creation, and in the state of integrity, he was exalted as head over angels and men; for which reason Paul calls him "the first-born of every creature;" but since the whole Scriptures proclaim, that he was clothed in flesh in order to become a Redeemer, it argues excessive temerity to imagine another cause or another end for it. The end for which Christ was promised from the beginning, is sufficiently known; it was to restore a fallen world, and to succour ruined men. Therefore under the law his image was exhibited in sacrifices, to inspire the faithful with a hope that God would be propitious to them, after he should be reconciled by the expiation of their sins. And as, in all ages, even before the promulgation of the law, the Mediator was never promised without blood, we conclude that he was destined by the eternal decree of God to purify the pollution of men; because the effusion of blood is an emblem of expiation. The prophets proclaimed and foretold him, as the future reconciler of God and men. As a sufficient specimen of all, we refer to that very celebrated testimony of Isaiah, where he predicts, that he should be smitten of God for the transgressions of the people, that the chastisement of their peace might be upon him; and that he should be a priest to offer up himself as a victim; that by his stripes others should be healed; and that because all men had gone astray, and been dispersed like sheep, it had pleased the Lord to afflict him and to lay on him the iniquities of all. As we are informed that Christ is particularly appointed by God for the relief of miserable sinners, all who pass these bounds are guilty of indulging a foolish curiosity. When he himself appeared in the world, he declared the design of his advent to be, to appease God and restore us from death to life. The apostles testified the same. Thus John, before he informs us that the Word was made flesh, mentions the defection of man. But our principal attention is due to Christ himself speaking of his own office. He says, "God so loved the world, that he gave his only begotten Son, that whosoever believeth in him should not perish, but have everlasting life." Again: "The hour is coming, and now is, when the dead shall hear the voice of the Son of God; and they that hear shall live." "I am the resurrection and the life; he that believeth in me, though he were dead, yet shall he live." Again: "The Son of man is come to save that which was lost." Again: "They that be whole need not a physician." There would be no end, if I meant to quote all the passages. The apostles with one consent call us back to this principle; for certainly, if he had not come to reconcile God, the honour of his priesthood would have been lost, for a priest is appointed as a Mediator to intercede between God and men: he could not have been our righteousness, because he was made a sacrifice for us, that God might not impute sins to us. Finally, he would have been despoiled of all the noble characters under which he is celebrated in the Scripture. This assertion of Paul would have no foundation: "What the law could not do, God, sending his own Son in the likeness of sinful flesh, and for sin, condemned sin in the flesh." Nor would there be any truth in what he teaches in another place, that "the kindness and love of God our Saviour towards man appeared" in the gift of Christ as a Redeemer. To conclude, the Scripture no where assigns any other end, for which the Son of God should choose to become incarnate, and should also receive this command from the Father, than that he might be made a sacrifice to appease the Father on our account. "Thus it is written, and thus it behoved Christ to suffer; and that repentance should be preached in his name." "Therefore doth my Father love me, because I lay down my life. This commandment have I received of my Father." "As Moses lifted up the serpent in the wilderness, even so must the Son of man be lifted up." Again: "Father, save me from this hour; but for this cause came I unto this hour." "Father, glorify thy Son." Where he clearly assigns, as the end of his assumption of human nature, that it was to be an expiatory sacrifice for the abolition of sins. For the same reason, Zacharias pronounces that he is come, according to the promise given to the fathers, "to give light to them that sit in the shadow of death." Let us remember that all these things are spoken of the Son of God, "in whom," according to the testimony of Paul, "are hidden all the treasures of wisdom and knowledge," and besides whom he glories in knowing nothing.

V. If any one object, that it is not evinced by any of these things, that the same Christ, who has redeemed men from condemnation, could not have testified his love to them by assuming their nature, if they had remained in a state of integrity and safety,—we briefly reply, that since the Spirit declares these two things, Christ's becoming our Redeemer, and his participation of the same nature, to have been connected by the eternal decree of God, it is not right to make any further inquiry. For he who feels an eager desire to know something more, not being content with the immutable appointment of God, shows himself also not to be contented with this Christ, who has been given to us as the price of our redemption. Paul not only tells us the end of his mission, but ascending to the sublime mystery of predestination, very properly represses all the licentiousness and prurience of the human mind, by declaring, that "the Father hath chosen us in Christ before the foundation of the world, and predestinated us to the adoption of children according to the good pleasure of his will, and made us accepted in his beloved Son, in whom we have redemption through his blood." Here the fall of Adam is certainly not presupposed, as of anterior date; but we have a discovery of what was decreed by God before all ages, when he determined to remedy the misery of mankind. If any adversary object again, that this design of God depended on the fall of man, which he foresaw, it is abundantly sufficient for me, that every man is proceeding with impious presumption to imagine to himself a new Christ, whoever he be that permits himself to inquire, or wishes to know, concerning Christ, any more than God has predestinated in his secret decree. And justly does Paul, after having been thus treating of the peculiar office of Christ, implore, on behalf of the Ephesians, the spirit of understanding, "that they may be able to comprehend what is the breadth, and length, and depth, and height; and to know the love of Christ, which passeth knowledge;" as though he would labour to surround our minds with barriers, that wherever mention is made of Christ, they may not decline in the smallest degree from the grace of reconciliation. Wherefore, since "this is" testified by Paul to be "a faithful saying, that Christ Jesus came into the world to save sinners," I gladly acquiesce in it. And since the same apostle in another place informs us, that "the grace, which is now made manifest by the gospel, was given us in Christ Jesus before the world began," I conclude that I ought to persevere in the same doctrine with constancy to the end. This modesty is unreasonably censured by Osiander, who in the present age has unhappily agitated this question, which a few persons had slightly touched before. He alleges a charge of presumption against those who deny that the Son of God would have appeared in the flesh, if Adam had never fallen, because this tenet is contradicted by no testimony of Scripture; as if Paul laid no restraint on such perverse curiosity, when, after having spoken of the accomplishment of our redemption by Christ, he immediately adds this injunction: "Avoid foolish questions." The frenzy of some, that have been desirous of appearing prodigiously acute, has proceeded to such a length as to question whether the Son of God could assume the nature of an ass. This monstrous supposition, which all pious persons justly abhor and detest, Osiander excuses under this pretext, that it is nowhere in Scripture expressly condemned; as if, when Paul esteems nothing valuable or worthy of being known but Christ crucified, he would admit an ass to be the author of salvation! Therefore he who in another place declares that Christ was appointed by the eternal decree of the Father as "the head over all," would never acknowledge any other who had not been appointed to the office of a Redeemer.

VI. But the principle which he boasts is altogether frivolous. He maintains that man was created in the image of God, because he was formed in the similitude of the future Messiah, that he might resemble him whom the Father had already decreed to clothe with flesh. Whence he concludes that if Adam had never fallen from his primitive integrity, Christ would nevertheless have become man. How nugatory and forced this is, all who possess a sound judgment readily perceive. But he supposes that he has been the first to discover wherein the Divine image consisted; namely, that the glory of God not only shone in those eminent talents with which man was endued, but that God himself essentially resided in him. Now, though I admit that Adam bore the Divine image, inasmuch as he was united to God, which is the true and consummate perfection of dignity, yet I contend that the similitude of God is to be sought only in those characters of excellence, with which God distinguished Adam above the other creatures. And that Christ was even then the image of God, is universally allowed; and therefore whatever excellence was impressed on Adam proceeded from this circumstance, that he approached to the glory of his Maker by means of his only begotten Son. Man, therefore, was made in the image of God, and was designed to be a mirror to display the glory of his Creator. He was exalted to this degree of honour by the favour of the only begotten Son; but I add, that this Son was a common head to angels as well as to men; so that the angels also were entitled to the same dignity which was conferred on man. And when we hear them called the "children of God," it would be unreasonable to deny that they have some resemblance to their Father. But if he designed his glory to be represented in angels as well as in men, and to be equally conspicuous in the angelic as in the human nature, Osiander betrays his ignorance and folly in saying that men were preferred to angels, because the latter did not bear the image of Christ. For they could not constantly enjoy the present contemplation of God, unless they were like him. And Paul teaches us that men are no otherwise renewed after the image of God, than that if they be associated with angels, they may be united together under one head. Finally, if we give credit to Christ, our ultimate felicity, when we shall be received into heaven, will consist in being conformed to the angels. But if Osiander may infer, that the primary exemplar of the Divine image was taken from the human nature of Christ, with the same justice may any other person contend, that Christ must have been a partaker of the nature of angels, because they likewise possess the image of God.

VII. Osiander, then, has no reason to fear, that God might possibly be proved a liar, unless the decree concerning the incarnation of his Son had been previously and immutably fixed in his mind. Because, though Adam had not fallen from his integrity, yet he would have resembled God just as the angels do; and yet it would not have been necessary on that account for the Son of God to become either a man or an angel. Nor has he any cause to fear this absurdity, that if God had not immutably decreed, before the creation of man, that Christ should be born, not as a Redeemer, but as the first man, he might lose his prerogative; whereas now he would not have become incarnate but for an accidental cause, that is, to restore mankind from ruin; so that he might thence infer, that Christ was created after the image of Adam. For why should he dread, what the Scripture so plainly teaches, that he was made like us in all things, sin excepted? whence also Luke hesitates not in his genealogy to call him "the son of Adam." I would also wish to know why Paul styles Christ "the second Adam," but because he was destined to become man, in order to extricate the posterity of Adam from ruin. If he sustained that capacity before the creation, he ought to have been called "the first Adam." Osiander boldly affirms, that because Christ was already foreknown as man in the Divine mind, therefore men were formed in his likeness. But Paul, by denominating him "the second Adam," places the fall, whence arises the necessity of restoring our nature to its primitive condition, in an intermediate point between the first original of mankind and the restitution which we obtain through Christ; whence it follows that the fall was the cause of the incarnation of the Son of God. Now, Osiander argues unreasonably and impertinently, that while Adam retained his integrity, he would be the image of himself, and not of Christ. On the contrary, I reply, that although the Son of God had never been incarnate, both the body and the soul of man would equally have displayed the image of God; in whose radiance it always appeared, that Christ was truly the head, possessing the supremacy over all. And thus we destroy that futile subtilty raised by Osiander, that the angels would have been destitute of this head, unless God had decreed to clothe his Son with flesh, even without any transgression of Adam. For he too inconsiderately takes for granted, what no wise man will concede, that Christ has no supremacy over angels, and that he is not their Prince, except in his human nature. But we may easily conclude, from the language of Paul, that, as the eternal Word of God, he is "the first-born of every creature;" not that he was created, or ought to be numbered among creatures, but because the holy state of the world, adorned as it was at the beginning with consummate beauty, had no other author; and that afterwards, as man, he was "the first begotten from the dead." For in one short passage he proposes to our consideration both these points—that all things were created by the Son, that he might have dominion over angels; and that he was made man, that he might become our Redeemer. Another proof of Osiander's ignorance is his assertion, that men would not have had Christ for their King, if he had not been incarnate; as though the kingdom of God could not subsist, if the eternal Son of God, without being invested with humanity, uniting angels and men in the participation of his glorious life, had himself held the supreme dominion! But he is always deceived, or rather bewilders himself, in this false principle, that the Church would have been destitute of a head, if Christ had not been manifested in the flesh; as if, while he was head over angels, he could not likewise by his Divine power preside over men, and by the secret energy of his Spirit animate and support them, like his own body, till they should be exalted to heaven, and enjoy the life of angels! These impertinencies, which I have thus far refuted, Osiander esteems as incontrovertible oracles. Inebriated by the charms of his own speculations, he is accustomed to express himself in the language of ridiculous triumph, without any sufficient cause. But he quotes one passage more, which he asserts to be conclusive beyond all the rest; that is, the prophecy of Adam, who, when he saw his wife, said, "This is now bone of my bone, and flesh of my flesh." But how does he prove this to be a prophecy? Because Christ, according to Matthew, attributes the same language to God; as though every thing that God has spoken by men contained some prophecy! Then Osiander may seek for prophecies in each of the precepts of the law, of which it is evident God was the author. Besides, Christ would have been a low and grovelling expositor, if he had confined himself to the literal sense. Because he is treating, not of the mystical union, with which he has honoured his Church, but only of conjugal fidelity; he informs us, that God had pronounced a husband and wife to be one flesh, that no one might attempt by a divorce to violate that indissoluble bond. If Osiander be displeased with this simplicity, let him censure Christ, because he did not conduct his disciples to a mystery, by a more subtile interpretation of the language of the Father. Nor does his delirious imagination obtain any support from Paul, who, after having said that "we are members of Christ's flesh," immediately adds, "this is a great mystery." For the apostle's design was, not to explain the sense in which Adam spoke, but, under the figure and similitude of marriage, to display the sacred union which makes us one with Christ. And this is implied in his very words; for when he apprizes us that he is speaking of Christ and the Church, he introduces a kind of correction to distinguish between the law of marriage and the spiritual union of Christ and the Church. Wherefore this futile notion appears destitute of any solid foundation. Nor do I think there will be any necessity for me to discuss similar subtilties; since the vanity of them all will be discovered from the foregoing very brief refutation. But this sober declaration will be amply sufficient for the solid satisfaction of the children of God; that "when the fulness of the time was come, God sent forth his Son, made of a woman, made under the law, to redeem them that were under the law."

NOTE

If you wish to read more of this text, you can find it in Calvin's Institutes of the Christian Religion, Book II.

www.ingramcontent.com/pod-product-compliance
Ingram Content Group UK Ltd.
Pitfield, Milton Keynes, MK11 3LW, UK
UKHW042018290726
14061UKWH00001BB/58

9 789360 510916

Enjoyed your Christian reading?

Don't end your introduction to Christian literature here.

Send a blank email to

thegoodchristian10@gmail.com

for access to Christian audiobooks.